The Eye Witness *Two*
Five Short Bible Novels

Biblical accounts as told by those who were there!

Douglas S. Malott

Copyright © 2014 Douglas S. Malott

All rights reserved.

ISBN-13: 978-1500268459

ISBN-10: 1500268453

DEDICATION

This book is dedicated to several people who have encouraged me in my pursuit of biblical understanding and application.

First, to my faithful parents, Doug and Marilu Malott, who instilled in me a great love of the scriptures by their example of devotion to reading its inspired words.

Second, to my beautiful and supportive wife Patti, who has encouraged me to read and study the scripture and most recently to write about its majestic beauty.

And third, the wonderful people at the Rock of Ages Christian Fellowship, where I have pastored for almost 34 years, who respectfully listen each week to my sermons and teaching and who have inspired me to handle the word of God carefully.

Thank you all for your support and encouragement!

CONTENTS

Dedication

Acknowledgments   vi

1   Story One: The Daring Synagogue Miracle   Pg. 11

2   Story Two: Tabatha Rises   Pg. 35

3   Story Three: Healing at Bethesda   Pg. 83

4   Story Four: The Leprosy Cure   Pg. 115

5   Story Five: The Glorious Shipwreck on the Island of Malta   Pg. 153

    About the Author   Pg. 185

ACKNOWLEDGMENTS

I would first like to thank my family for their support and encouragement in trying such a project as this book effort. My wife Patti and all four of my grown children were very positive about the idea, even though it seemed like a lot of work.

Next, I would like to thanks numerous members of my congregation at Rock of Ages Christian Fellow for their encouragement. Originally the story ideas were presented as either additions to sermon outlines or dramatically presented monologues which I read to the church on Sunday mornings. Each presentation was met with very positive feedback and the request for me to consider compiling them in a written collection and making them available in published form.

Finally, the finished product could not have been presented without the tedious work of editing. I was fortunate enough to have talented family members available who patiently read and corrected all of the content: Kudos to Susan Matteson, and Patti Malott.

Douglas S. Malott

INTRODUCTION

In the following pages of the 'The Eye Witness Two', familiar biblical accounts are presented and described in 'short novel' form. The technical term for this kind of short novel is 'novelette'. A novelette is generally a story of approximately 7,000 words to 17,000 words. Each of the five stories in this second volume of 'The Eye Witness' series fit into this word count and thus are 'novelettes' by traditional definition. In these Bible accounts the same effort is made as in the first collection of The Eye Witness short stories. The Bible accounts are told by either unnamed fictionalized characters or real characters, whose personal life is enhanced fictionally in order to give and eye witness account to the events!

With added background information and historical perspective brought into the actual bible text you will experience dramatic adaptation of biblical history and watch the scripture text come alive with added 'personality' and realistic 'color' commentary. Each event is presented in plausible adaptation that gives the reader more personal involvement in the stories we all love to read.

Story One

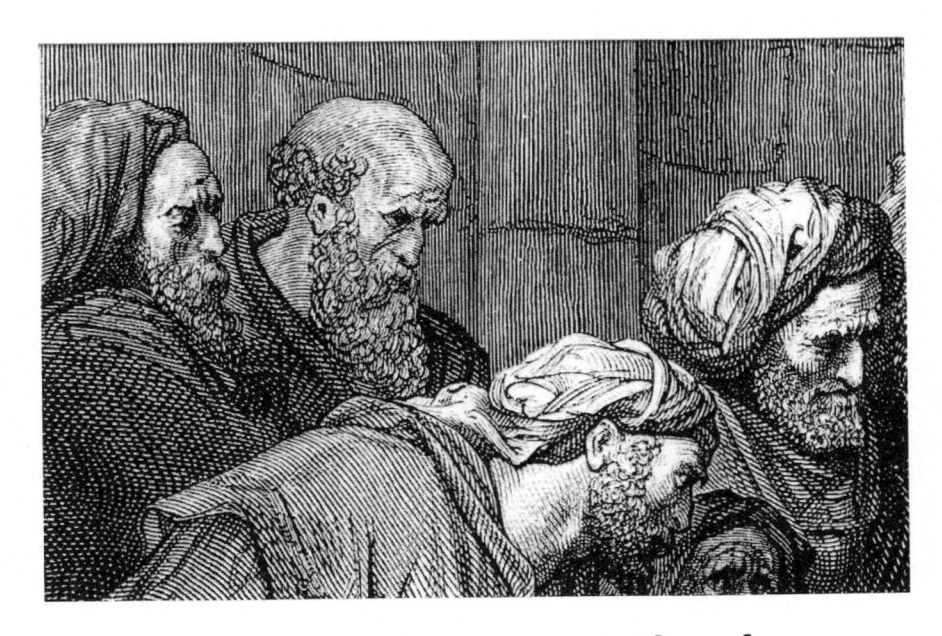

The Daring Synagogue Miracle

The Daring Synagogue Miracle
(Based on Matthew 12:9–14; Mark 3:1–6; Luke 6:6–11)

Chapter One

Exquisite Joy

As I stand here surrounded by my fellow Hebrew brethren, I must concentrate with all the will power I can find to contain my joy and laughter. After all, such expression would prove to be improper for a traditional synagogue worship experience. Although I am on the verge of bursting with excitement and delight, I have chosen to respect my fellow worshippers and keep my internally raucous emotions calm and contained. Looking out over the drably colored head coverings, veils and prayer shawls that surround me in every direction, I can only guess as to the depth of devotion that each person in this hallowed chamber is feeling at the moment. For in the close quarters of the synagogue, every Hebrew man must respect the reverent and solemn atmosphere and not risk any undue demonstration that might be interpreted as bringing disrespect to God and His sacred law. Thus, standing among the men of our Jewish community to pay reverence to the Law of God is pressure enough to control my emotions. Even with such exuberance surging in my soul, I dare not choose to appear frivolous in the synagogue meeting. This, however, is not easily done today! For myself, my faithful wife of many years and several close friends who are present in this great hall, the undercurrent of ecstasy is barely controllable!

Since our very first synagogue meeting three years ago, my wife and I have faithfully practiced our Jewish faith and synagogue worship. I remember clearly the thrill that came to my heart when our Jewish community first realized that we had met the minimal requirement for establishing our own synagogue. As required by Temple law, a local synagogue could only be organized with the commitment of no fewer than 10 faithful Jewish men who would gather for regular meeting. With the growing Jewish religious community, here in Capernaum, it had not been hard to achieve this milestone, once word had gotten out to the religious Jewish population of the city. And thus we were able to make our synagogue an official gathering place for the many who desired to worship Jehovah in the public setting. Over these three years we had added to our numbers and also regularly welcomed many Romans and Greeks into our worship experience. These Greek and Roman gentiles, who regularly met with us became known as *noadiches,* or "God-fearers" to all of us of Hebrew decent. They needed to simply acknowledge the God of Israel as the only true God and the worshipping community would welcome them. So it was that we conducted weekly meetings with the blessing of the Chief Temple Priests.

Men, women and children alike attended these meetings weekly, however only the men were allowed to stand nearest the 'bema' or platform at the front-center of the room. On this 'bema' or platform, was the *holy chest,* which contained the scroll of the Law and the reading desk, from where the scripture was read for all to hear. Women and children both stood in the back of the chamber or in the upper level balcony and watched the proceedings quietly and reverently from that vantage point, while men only read the holy scripture and engaged in discussion and teaching concerning its timeless truth and applications.

So it was that in this atmosphere of fervency and religious zeal, just over the fingertips of my own raised and worshipful hand, I could cast a glimpse toward my wife, who, in the small balcony just above and to the right of me, was showing similar signs of bottled up euphoric joy. I could tell as I gazed toward her shining countenance that she too was struggling to remain calm and respectful of the worship proceedings taking place around and beneath her. All the while I knew she was rehearsing and savoring the gladness that surged through her spirit and of course was still surging through mine as well. In fact, as I describe this scene and think back over what caused our glorious joy, looking up just beyond the slight rhythmic movement of my own outstretched arm, our eyes meet and we greet each other with sparkling eyes and warm tears of joy. We are still barely able to contain the exuberance that bubbles behind our constrained smiles.

What is the cause of such joy you might ask? What brings this barely controlled bliss to the surface of our hearts, you wonder? What would be the source of such binding ecstasy between two aging and long married people? Well, let me tell you our story, and in doing so may our God be praised and His Messiah exalted!

Chapter Two

The Pain Begins

It had been many years since that fateful day of tragedy. The injury that would debilitate my future came during the early spring planting season. Tulia and I had not been married but two shorts years and having just secured a small piece of land on the outskirts of Capernaum, my wife and I were working hard at clearing the soil of rock and boulders. Our small piece of land looked southeast from the ragged basalt foothills that rimmed the city to the north and west. On most days we could view the glimmer of the northern end of the Lake of Galilee as it lay just beyond the city from our vantage point. Capernaum was a busy fishing village and regular starting point for small sailing vessels that ventured out on the Lake. It was also a main connection by road between The Great Sea to the west and Damascus to the northeast. It was one of many villages around the Lake of Galilee that provided a hub of fishing, agricultural and social activity for the local people who had lived there for many generations. Since we had no connection to the fishing business we concentrated on our farming and herding duties. Toiling in the earth was necessary in order to prepare the unyielding soil in our area for planting small crops of barley and other grains. This small scale farming effort and the work that went along with home ownership soon pre-occupied most of our time making our connection to Capernaum mostly one of dedication to our Jewish worship and the local synagogue. And of course, preparing the soil for planting was a top priority if we were to live off the produce and have some extra to sell at the local markets.

Maneuvering rocks and boulders out of the soil and away from the planting space was no small task. This, for two people, even though newly married and still without children, took many long days of backbreaking labor. To simplify the effort and also provide some sense of security to our small dwelling and the plot of dirt we called home, we had decided to arrange the larger rocks and boulders along the outer limits of our property. Rather than carrying them any great distance away from the land, these stones would make a very satisfactory stone wall to mark out the safe confines of our simple but very adequate home. It would also provide some limited security from any unwanted critters and people.

It was during this stone moving project that the accident occurred and the curse of many difficult years had begun. Working on the last 15 cubits of stone placement, before the wall met the back corner of the house, I was laboring especially hard to get several large and heavy boulders into place on the top of the wall. My wife, Tulia, stood by watching as several neighbor friends assisted me in lifting these last few stones into a small cart that would be pushed and pulled alongside the remaining length of wall and permit these rocks to be lifted carefully to their final resting place. Once the cart had been maneuvered into place by the hardy group of workers, three of us who were the strongest of the work crew, lifted a particularly heavy stone onto the wall's surface. Thinking it to be secure we had released it to its spot with a thud and then sank to our knees in relief, exhaustion and dust-caked perspiration. Exchanging glances and congratulations we had sat still just long enough to catch our breath and decide what was next to be done. It was then, that without warning, several smaller rocks gave way under the weight of the larger one and set this grand stone piece at the top of the pile into motion just above my head and right shoulder. All three of us attempted to scramble with desperate effort away from the wall, but since I was the one closer to the piled up stones, my escape was too slow and too late. After just a few seconds of surprised movement I was caught by the plummeting boulder and its extreme weight.

Scraping, grinding and sliding down the jagged stone pile, this granite like hulk came crashing and crushing its way down on my right wrist and hand. The pain was immediate and overwhelming. It was all I could do to keep myself from losing consciousness and passing out on the spot. My two friends darted to my side while Tulia rushed toward me, screaming as she came. Fighting against the pain and the loss of blood to my head I grabbed the rugged edge of this huge rock with my free hand and leaned as hard I could into its side. My two helpers and Tulia joined me in the pushing as we groaned and shrieked, straining to dislodge the stone from my lower arm. With great energy and effort the four of us were able to tilt this hulking stone up on one end just enough to release my arm and hand. With the pressure of the rock gone I painfully pulled my limp arm, wrist and fingers clear of the stone and watched through tightly squinting eye lids as the stone was left to drop back to its place. With the jabbing pain finally relieved I exhaled one long breath and laid backward on the ground; the gritty crushing stone sitting on one side of my shaking body and my weeping wife on the other.

Several minutes of light headedness passed before the throbbing of my wrist brought me up to my elbow to look at the damage. My friends, as well as Tulia, gathered close and joined my horrified gaze down at the damage limb. Blood oozed from several punctures in my palm and wrist area. The skin, in several areas on my lower arm was blotched pale white from the weight of the rock and was slow to return to flesh color because of the damage to the tissue under the skin. I could tell by the pain and loss of mobility in my lower extremity that I had broken several bones of both my hand and my arm. The jabbing pain and waves of nausea gave me little time to assess the silent creeping fear that would later grip my mind openly. At that point all I could think about was finding a more private place to lay down and proceed with nursing my wounds. Having use of my elbow but not my hand or wrist I struggled to my knees and then to my wobbly feet while slowly pulling my lower arm into the cradle of my other hand. As I stood, I was immediately met by several strong supportive arms and the outstretched hands of my still weeping wife. Leaning on those around me, Tulia, guided us slowly as we proceeded to the house. It was there where Tulia would do her best to patiently wash, sanitize and wrap my damaged arm.

Pain and discomfort characterized my days for many months after that fateful afternoon. We had hoped that with time and some limited physician care my hand and wrist would regain its function and mobility. **It did not.** Although the outer damage eventually reversed itself and the bone structure largely healed over the months, the internal damage proved to be permanent and debilitating. My right hand, wrist and lower arm became paralyzed and in time began to wither and look grotesquely curled and twisted. Any work I engaged in proved to be tedious and humiliating for me as I had to lean more heavily on my wife to get things done around the house and on the land. As well, any additional carpentry work and other menial labor, which I had been accustomed to doing for additional income was largely out of the question at that point. It would remain so until I would be able to readjust to working with my LEFT hand and arm and living with a permanently paralyzed right hand and wrist. Although Tulia and I made do and did the best we could under the circumstances, my paralysis became a daily reminder of our ongoing disability and the dramatic changes that had altered our course in life, tarnishing our future dreams. So it was, that when the mercy of God brought to us another fateful day, we were completely unprepared for its glorious results.

Chapter Three

The Synagogue Confrontation

Visiting the Synagogue was a weekly routine for us as it was for all good Jews. Beside the Sabbath visit, we regularly attended synagogue on the 2nd and 5th day of each week. It was during these segregated worship experiences that both men, on the lower floor of the chamber, and women and children, in the balcony above or back of the room, would gather. Each and every time we met, the *Shema,* our confession of faith, was recited by all. This sacred confession, composed of passages of the Torah which included sections from the Pentateuch books of Deuteronomy, chapter 6 and 11 and Numbers, chapter 15, served to remind us constantly of our need to obey God's Law. Also, many prayers were offered during our meeting time and Holy Scripture was read aloud making sure we covered the entire Law of God once every three years. Included as well, in the formal meeting was an address or teaching by any one of a number of qualified leaders. This particular portion of the synagogue service was adjusted from time to time to allow for visitors or laymen to address the crowd, engage in limited debate over doctrine or local concerns or simply share any personal testimonies of God's work.

It was in this regular weekly setting that we had first noticed the Prophet from Galilee. Jesus, who was originally from the small village of Nazareth, had arrived some months prior with a large contingent of disciples and He and his followers had attended synagogue worship regularly over these months after first coming to Capernaum to live. It appeared to us that Capernaum had become an ideally central location for his preaching and travel. As the weeks and months progressed, however, an undercurrent of concern and suspicion had developed among many of our leaders concerning this man Jesus. Some of His unorthodox ways, mannerisms, the people He associated with, and His message made the leading Pharisees very nervous. Many Pharisees from the surrounding cities and villages had made regular visits to observe the prophet Jesus and his disciples. Indeed some from Jerusalem, the Holy City, had even taken up residence here in Capernaum in an apparent effort to keep a close eye on this man from Galilee.

At the time Tulia and I were not concerned. In our regular exposure to this preacher and his disciples in and around the Synagogue, He had said nothing that caused us any real concern. Whether or not he was the messiah, as some claimed, we did not know. We simple enjoyed his teaching in the synagogue and hearing of the miracles that many said He performed regularly as He traveled.

Although needing a miracle ourselves, we had not seen any of His miracles, largely due to my handicap and how it kept us confined to Capernaum and the immediate area. Also, the stress of making ends meet on a daily basis as well as our regular involvement in synagogue service and worship filled almost all of our time.

It was a typical Sabbath that fateful day of our personal encounter with Jesus. Having arrived at Synagogue early we soon were joined by several hundred men and women who were crowding into the building with us. Finding my way into the room brought me across the view of Jesus, who was already seated near the front. We exchanged pleasant glances briefly, as I held my paralyzed arm to my body so as not to be clumsy and bump any men who were already in their places. The other men were crowding into the lower chamber of the hall and the wives, of course, were making their way to the balcony above or to seats in the back of the room. They would participate, but only at a distance and without interrupting the order of service on the floor below them. Soon the atmosphere was full of chanting, prayers and scripture reading. And as was expected, the service made its regular progression toward the centerpiece of the entire affair; *the public address*.

At first, as the room settled into a more somber and quiet tone, no one came forward. The synagogue leaders, in the front of the room, were preoccupied with their own personal discussions and from my view point seemed a bit agitated by the presence of several individuals in the crowd. It appeared to me that those who were causing the greatest concern were Temple leaders who had traveled here from Jerusalem. They were not usually in attendance and so I assumed they were here to watch the prophet from Nazareth. A quiet hum of conversation began to hang over the whole of the people as this delay continued. I assumed we were waiting for the synagogue leader to step forward and begin some doctrinal debate or introduce another person to the crowd who would address us. So, I was taken back when a man in the front of the room stood to his feet, turned slightly to address the entire group gathered there and spoke out over the heads of the seated men. He appeared to be one of the new comers to our place of worship.

"Is it lawful to heal on the Sabbath?" he asked to no one in particular, speaking out over the crowd.

As his voice broke over the low murmuring of voices, an uneasy silence slowly filled the entire chamber. In my mind, it appeared that the new comer's address had a certain calculation to it, it was as if the synagogue leaders knew beforehand that it would happen. In fact, thinking back on that day now, I'm sure their delay was part of the plan to pose a challenge to the prophet. Everyone's attention quickly became focused to the front of the columned synagogue hall. All eyes soon were focused on the speaker.

"Is it lawful to heal on the Sabbath?" he repeated with continued agitation and strength.

This time, however, the question was directed not at the crowd but toward Jesus, who was still sitting quietly in his original place near the front and waiting with the rest of us for the address to begin. This particular kind of question was not an unusual one. These kinds of enquiries could be made on a regular basis and would make for very heated debate and discussion. We were accustomed to such debate as this. It was, however, unusual to have such questions used to aggressively challenge and almost threaten an opposing itinerate prophet, like this man from Galilee!

Chapter Four

The Unexpected Answer

Slowly, without fanfare or emotion Jesus stood to his feet. With his head covering and long dark hair framing his face he turned slightly to his left to face the Pharisee who had first asked the question. It was clear to the entire crowd that He intended to offer an answer to this man and address the previous question. However, before doing so, turning slowly back in the *opposite* direction, *away* from the man who had made the verbal challenge, he cast a glance in my direction. Catching my eye and smiling ever so faintly, He nodded his head slightly and then looked back at His inquirer and prepared to respond. Although facing his challenger, Jesus now directed himself to the entire synagogue throng by posing his own question for us to ponder.

"What man among you, if he had a sheep that fell into a pit on the Sabbath, wouldn't take hold of it and lift it out? He asked, matching question for question, in return.

This brought a ripple of sound from the crowd. First, from the gathered men and then from the woman, who watched from their distant perches. All of us present understood His meaning and from the amount of energy that instantly rose to the surface in the place, it seemed clear to me that most were inclined to agree with this prophet from Galilee. Indeed all of us, as hardworking people, knew that the Law of God and its many precepts would allow for such practical assistance to care for one's herd or flock in such emergency settings. Now, we waited to see how our visiting prophet would apply this common sense answer to the original question of healing on the Sabbath.

"A man is worth far more than a sheep, so it is lawful to do what is good on the Sabbath." Jesus continued with his response and then waited.

At this additional comment, the questioner and his group of supporters fell silent where they stood. His answer seemed to surprise these who were taking it on themselves to protect the Sabbath. Their question had been intended as a trap, but His answer provided no such trap! However, in their silence, they betrayed their inactivity by showing continued visible hostility toward Jesus of Nazareth and proceeded to stand their ground in waiting for more explanation to their original question. It was at this juncture that the meeting made a drastic shift from discussion and debate to dramatic action. Now, to my surprise, turning to his right, Jesus again faced in my direction. And to my utter amazement he began pointing to me and gesturing with his hand that I should stand to my feet.

"Stand up so all of us can see you!" He asked me directly.

At this request from the prophet the room fell almost deathly silent. All voices were muted and any movement among the crowd waned quickly, serving to create a completely hushed atmosphere. My attention like everyone else's was now captured by the exchange of words at the front of the room. Sitting about three rows back from the front, I slowly, with much trepidation, stood to my feet. In doing so I was forced to awkwardly hold my paralyzed arm to my side and make it all too noticeable. Grasping my limp and burdensome arm had become a mindless habit for me over time as I daily attempted to make my way through life with some semblance of normalcy. But, this kind of exposure felt very abnormal! Once standing to my feet, I could see that every eye in the chamber was trained on me. Even the whole of the balcony of women seemed to be leaning over the front barrier to watch me as I stood in the crowd. And of course, there, pressing herself to the front of the balcony edge was my Tulia, wide eyed and terrified, looking out over the whole development on the floor below.

Turning my gaze back to Jesus, I noticed that his eyes were no longer soft and inviting. At his earlier request for me to stand, I had seen an inviting and accepting gaze, but now his face was sterner and his eyes were fiery and piercing. It seemed to me they even glinted with a hint of sadness. He was now looking out over the crowd and in particular watching the crowd as it focused its attention toward those Pharisees who had challenged him with the question about the Sabbath. This development seemed to please those Pharisees who were visiting as representatives of the High Priest and the Temple. This kind of public sparing made for the best opportunity to humiliate an opponent and so as the preacher continued, these religious leaders prepared for what they thought would be their victory. Little did they know!

"I ask you all again: Is it lawful on the Sabbath to do what is good or to do what is evil, to save life or to destroy it?" he repeated to the whole chamber and in particular to those who were His detractors.

I stood silently, while watching and listening to this verbal and philosophical tug of war developing between Jesus and these pharisaical leaders. The tension in the chamber was becoming stronger as everyone seemed to almost hold their breath in anticipation and concern. I was not sure why I had been asked to stand and as the tension increased in the atmosphere of the room, I was beginning to think this whole episode might be a big mistake. I wondered momentarily, if it might be better to just sit back down and not participate. In spite of the growing tension and my internal questioning, I remained standing and chose to purposely fix my attention on the face of the prophet.

"Stretch out your hand" he now spoke to me, breaking the tension with His words of authority.

The words seem to float across the room toward me in a slow lilting motion. "Stretch out your hand" he had said. This was something that I had not been able to do for many years and yet Jesus had just invited me to do that very thing. Could I stretch out my hand? Where would the strength come from to lift my lifeless limb into the open air for all of these people in the room to see? As I silently questioned myself, the words of Jesus began gathering additional swiftness and pressed further into my mind; they no longer floated but darted and pushed themselves into my thinking. "Stretch out your Hand" he had said. Something in the authority of his voice, now prodded me to do my best to cooperate with his daring command. So, very deliberately, with the help of my left hand, I began to pull my right arm up and out to the front of my body, knowing full well that with this kind of movement the dysfunction of my withered arm would be obvious to all. I strained only for a very brief moment at this unfamiliar action. As I did so, instantaneous rushes of energy and strength shot down my arm from my shoulder to my fingers. Reoccurring waves of tingling and heat intermittently washed over my entire right side as my wrist joint and finger joints began loosening and flexing. Quite without any ability on my part, my entire arm was being energized as muscle and tissue discovered their new found freedom.

My fingers, hand, wrist and lower arm were being restored as my arm was lifted. Now my entire right arm seemed to be feather like, almost without weight or bulk. Fingers, hand, wrist, and forearm lifted without additional effort. Full motion of movement took control of bone, muscle and joint, all the way to my very fingertips. Limp and twisted tissue straightened and swelled with vitality, as we watched.

And as it did, I could hear the crowd around and above me gasp in startled amazement. Their reaction was muffled only because I became preoccupied with my own astonishment and emotion. Even the view of Jesus and his opponents faded slightly in the moment, as the emotion in my heart and mind went from instant shock to being filled with awe and praise toward God. Being far too overcome with excitement, I could not find the means to turn and gaze in the direction of my beloved wife. As it turned out, that did not matter, because through the chorus of cheers coming from the gasping onlookers I could hear her voice ringing out toward me. Calling, crying and laughing; she too was transfixed in praise and gratitude to God almighty.

After several minutes of being lost in my own wonder, I was quickly brought back to reality as I realized that I had now been surrounded by friends and well-wishers who were clamoring to see my restored arm and hand and join me with their own praise to God. In the clamor and joyous confusion that progressively engulfed me, I could soon see my wife above me crying tears of joy as she looked down, seeing me trapped in the excitement and dismay of the crowd. As well, I could still see that Jesus and several of His disciples were still lingering in the chamber, standing near one of the distant supporting stone columns, approvingly watching the entire scene develop in front of them. If it had not been for the crush of the crowd and my supporting friends I would have rushed to the feet of this prophet of Galilee and poured out my own immense approval!

In the closing moments of that particular synagogue meeting I eventually was able to move to the back of the room and stand waiting for Tulia to join me. Once she did we were both then able to watch the final scene of tension between this Jesus of Nazareth and the troubled Pharisees come to an abrupt end. Jesus, quietly receiving respect, handshakes and compliments from many in the chamber, stood off to the side of the room, so as not to disrupt the jubilant scene taking place around me. At the same time the small group of visiting Pharisee leaders argued among themselves and eventually stormed from the building in a huff of anger.

In watching their departure, I was sure their intentions were not good. No doubt they were intent on bringing a negative report to those waiting in Jerusalem; to those who had sent them on their suspicious journey. These legalistic religious leaders had been dispatched to Capernaum in an attempt to expose and embarrass the itinerate preacher and in the end he had turned their effort back onto their own heads with the embarrassment of a public gift of healing! Their plots that day had been silenced by the healing of my withered hand; but I felt sure that tomorrow or the next day or some day in the immediate future they would plot again against this Man of God, this Messiah sent from heaven.

For me, their anger was incidental and even foolish! Undeniably, in one divine moment of time, my life had been changed, my dreams had been restored and a future that I had deemed lost forever, had been given back to me. And at that moment, with the full weight of this new reality billowing over me, I could do nothing but weep, wiping tears of joy from my face with BOTH HANDS!

The End.

Story Two

Tabitha Rises

Douglas S. Malott

Tabitha Rises
(Based on Acts 9:32-43)

Chapter 1

View of Joppa 1893 by Bishop John H. Vincent; Rev. James W. Lee

A City Awaits

I am Joppa, a small but busy Israeli port city, situated on the beautifully scenic Mediterranean Sea. I look west upon the Sea's most eastern expanse, a view that has been both glorious and frightening as the centuries have come and gone. My story in history and in the bible is directly linked to several people, but none as important as the story of one women who made her home among my cloistered streets and back alley ways. This woman, Tabitha, whose name means 'Gazelle' was one of my finest, most genuine of people and as such would impact those who lived within my humble walls with her fruitful life, as well as her untimely death. Death was no stranger to my historic streets and plundered dwellings, as many a crushing foot had overrun my walls and bulwarks to conquer my people. So, in the general course of middle eastern history, this Tabitha's death should have raised little notice or concern; but, this death would prove to be uncommon and indeed, short lived! For this death, although very real and sorrowful, would be miraculously reversed, and in its reversal would announce a drastic change for those living within my ancient stone barriers!

I have been a fortified port city overlooking this eastern portion of the Mediterranean Sea for more than 2,000 years and as such was one of the world's most ancient and strategic small cities. The earliest inhabitants I saw gather here, settled some 7,500 years before the days of which I am describing here. The naturally rocky shoreline, with its jutting and protruding rock outcroppings, made for a well-protected port of entry but an ill-suited harbor. Thus, when ships with visitors or goods and materials arrived at this ancient landing point to be off loaded, they usually had to anchor offshore and send their cargo into my port area in longboats and dinghies. Rising quickly, some 130 feet, from the lapping waves of my sand and rock shoreline, I also command a view of the north and south coastline.

This view up and down the water's edge perpetually provided natural protection and made me a very attractive place for military presence and defense. As the military hoards swarmed over me and trampled my fair dwellings and private streets and passageways, pain and suffering were the common denominator that linked all of my people to the past, present and the future.

As a small but vital port area I was the target of conquerors throughout the centuries because of my strategic location between Asia Minor and the North African continent and Europe. Significant world powers of the day and oppressive regional powers as well vied for control over me for many centuries. I was a pristine treasure on a rugged and foreboding shoreline. Controlling me, controlled a major entry point to all of ancient Israel. The Ancient Egyptians made their presence felt within my walled protections, as well as the Greeks of Alexander the Great. Seleucid commanders, Maccabean rebels and the unconventional and fierce Romans all took their turns conquering and controlling my strategic oasis on the Great Sea.

I have watched the centuries pass with grief and foreboding as my victimized inhabitants suffered at the hands of those who simply wanted to control my physical attributes for their selfish goals. Together, my honored residents and I longed for a better time, an expression of life and liberty, free of bloodshed and full of generosity and joy! As the long centuries and their generations came and went, we resisted hopelessness and choose to yearn for lasting peace and prosperity. As it turned out, our longings were finally realized, but none of us were prepared for how the fulfillment would arrive!

It was from my harbor and its busy commerce that central Israel received much of its needed goods and supplies. The larger cities of Caesarea, to the north 25 miles and the Holy City, Jerusalem, 35 miles over the Judean hills to the east, depended much on the movement of people, provisions and materials to and from my bejeweled metropolis, situated perfectly on the turquoise waters of the Great Western Sea. To the north stretched the Plain of Sharon and to the south, the Plain of Philistia. I stood ready to channel people and commerce to the east as well as the north and south of Israel.

As an ancient city, I had enjoyed a rich association with famous biblical leaders over the centuries. In the settlement of the Promised Land, the tribe of Dan was given the territory that included me as a seaport. It was from my blessed harbor that King Solomon, of Israel, brought the Cedars of Lebanon to build the first great temple of the God of Israel. Later, Ezra the priest, supervised the rebuilding of the Second Temple of God and again, timbers for its construction came through my gates and roadways. And of course, it was from my port that the prophet Jonah first fled from the presence of God, hoping to escape the call to prophecy against the great city of Nineveh.

Although, conquered and reconquered over the centuries by northern and southern kingdoms alike, as the valued Joppa, I soon found myself under the direct rule of the ever expanding Roman Empire and its local puppet king, the evil and scheming King Herod. During these tumultuous periods of upheaval and change, I had managed to survive and at times even thrive in my seafaring and maritime duties to the nation of Israel. Under the current rule of King Herod the region had prospered, even if its inhabitants were constantly suspicious and leery of his influence and power. This unpredictable ruler was at the same time a curse and a blessing to my existence!

Life within my secluded gates had been largely removed from the most recent and troubling events that had captured the attention of the nation of Israel and its people. There had been many such events in the recent decades that had resulted in bloodshed and heartache for my people but this most recent episode was proving to leave a profound impression on the entire nation. It would prove to bring unusual and fearful changes to Hebrew religious life in general. It seemed that as hard as the nation's religious leaders had tried, they could not stop the spread of a new religious fervor that appeared to be finding expression and fertile ground in cities, towns and villages all across Judea and Samaria. In the previous year a tragic and violent end had come to a man called Jesus, after 3 ½ years of public ministry. This man from Galilee had turned the nation of Israel on its ear with fervent preaching, performing powerful miracles, healing the sick and diseased and confronting the Jewish religious leaders for their shallow and empty adherence to the Law of God. All of this had brought great hope to many in Israel but in the end resulted in a heartrending and bloody crucifixion of this Jesus, at the hands of both the Roman and the Jewish religious leaders.

It had been expected that the gruesome death of Jesus, whom some called the Christ, would bring an end to the movement that had formed around him. Many Jewish loyalist had hoped to scatter his disciples and bring a semblance of peace and control back to the Hebrew leaders of the Sanhedrin. However, this had not happened at all! Instead, reports of this man's resurrection and his numerous appearances to his disciples had emboldened these followers to continue preaching the message that this godly messenger had brought to the nation. Jesus of Nazareth was now being proclaimed in Jerusalem and the surrounding regions as the promised and risen Messiah!

It would be the message of the Messiah, brought by travelers and believers escaping the persecution that had erupted in Jerusalem, that would capture the heart and mind of our godly

Tabitha. This servant of God, a beautiful expression of faithful innocence and humble enthusiasm, would experience not only a personal encounter with the living Christ, but her own taste of death and her resurrection at the hands of an Apostle of Jesus would propel the message of good news through every quarter of my needy community. This woman and her story would change the very atmosphere over my ancient chiseled walls and transform many of my inhabitants in ways that would never be reversed.

Chapter 2

Joppa Harbor – 1893 - by Bishop John H. Vincent; Rev. James W. Lee

Unwelcome Business

This Tabitha, a Jewess, whose Greek name was Dorcas, lived in the heart of my business district as part of a growing Christian community of believers. She had not always been a follower of the Messiah, Jesus, but had faithfully served the Jewish community and the local synagogue with great fervor. In the days prior to her widowhood, she and her husband had been instrumental in giving leadership to the local Jewish people. He, by teaching and serving as an intermediary between the officials of King Herod and the local synagogue in Joppa. She, by giving many hours of help and support to the needy with her gifts of sewing, weaving and tailoring. This talented women of means bought cloth and fine fabric that were brought into the city from many places around the shores of the Mediterranean Sea and fashioned exquisite robes, tunics, scarves and other items, many of which were given away to those of lesser means.

Widowhood, although common among the families of Israel but never desired, was served to Tabitha by an unfortunate turn of events. Tabitha's husband, Elian, had been at the center of negotiations with a Treasurer of King Herod's court about taxes that were owed to the palace. Several Synagogue leaders and local businessmen had been meeting with the officials from Jerusalem to settle a disagreement over the amount expected to be paid. As always, the issue of taxation was a volatile topic and many times cooler heads failed to prevail in the negotiations and bloodshed had erupted as a result. This episode would be no different.

It had become clear in the deliberations that the Treasurer and his delegation intended to exact more taxes than was necessary from the Synagogue and the community of Jews. Their intent was to collect the prescribed amount, even at the risk of violence. This intent was soon understood by the local leaders and as resistance developed, many of the more zealous, anti-Herod factions combined forces in an attempt to prevent the unjust collection of the tax money. So it was, in the open air market place meeting, where both parties had been arguing and debating the tax liability; a small group of these local zealots seeking to defend the rights of the common people, angrily attacked the King's delegation.

I remember the day well! A gray sky seemed to hang low over my golden yellow stone walls and unsuspecting thoroughfares. Tensions were running high and it seemed the whole of the city nervously waited for the matter to be settled. These matters of religious and political concerns always spread their web-like fibers throughout the whole of the city and brought emotions to the surface where anything could and did happen. In the market square, near the east gate of the city, the opposing groups were meeting with the primary leaders exchanging heated words and expressions in an emotional wrestling match that was clear to all who stood in the shadows awaiting the outcome. Emotion-filled words and gestures were flung like invisible weapons from both sides.

The King's Treasurer, a tall imposing man with deep set eyes and neatly trimmed beard, sat at one side of a small table with four attendants standing just behind and about a dozen armed guards from the palace standing behind them, their backs to the open east gate. Elian and one other leading member of the business community sat across the table making the case for my people and the whole of Joppa. Tabitha, who certainly could have been there that day given her business expertise, had been forbidden by her husband from making an appearance, given the danger that no doubt would develop. Elian, a fair minded man and thus well respected in the community, had come alone to these negotiations. His presence would mean that honesty and a reasonable attitude would dominate the conversations. Behind them stood several groupings of local business men and community leaders listening intently to the ongoing conversation in front of them and hoping that generous minds would prevail and those given to more violent expressions would hold themselves in check. The air was stagnant and motionless and the gray sky continued to impose its gloom on the whole area.

It became clear after a grueling hour or so of emotional debate, that the King's delegation was not about to be persuaded to accept less revenue and was intending to move with force to secure their demands and leave the city, if need be. It seemed that the Treasurer, attendants and the entire guard unit were at the ready with nervous hands and twitchy fingers on swords, spears and whips. Those at the table were painfully aware of this slowly developing tension but could do little to stop its escalation. In particular Elian, who had come hoping for the best, saw that the opposition was preferring possible brutality over any sensible compromise.

It was then, as the observed show of force was developing, that from the back of the crowd, behind Elian and the other local leaders, a large stone came hurtling out over the heads of the observers. Its calculated course of flight brought it slamming into the neck and shoulder of the Treasurer as he sat at the table. The force of the blow sent him and his chair tumbling backward into the dirt and dust of the market place floor. In the brief moment it took him to teeter backward, hit the ground and roll onto his back, blood could be seen beginning to ooze and run down the side of his jaw and neck onto his tunic and then to the soil beneath him. This was all it took for the guards to lurch into action. Like uncoiling, lunging snakes, two of them sprang toward the Treasurer to help bring him to his feet while all of the others drew their swords or readied their spears and rushed toward the opposition sitting and standing across the table.

At the sight of the Treasurer's bloodied face and neck and the guards advancing toward the Jewish negotiators, pandemonium broke out across the open market. Now a hail of stones came raining down on the Kings delegation and hundreds of both participators and onlookers alike scattered in all directions to escape the developing confrontation. Screaming voices of fear and anger rang out, echoing back and forth against the market's stone walls. Dust from pounding feet rose quickly in the swirling air of the market place and added a murky dimension to the already eerie scene.

In spite of the potential for prolonged combative action, to the relief of all, the guards concentrated on securing the King's Treasurer, collecting the tax money from beside the table and dispelling the crowd from the immediate area rather than taking out any vengeance on the crowd.

As the noise in the market settled back to normal and the dust settled enough for a more complete assessment to be made of the damages and injuries, it became clear that not everyone had escaped the turmoil that had engulfed the market that afternoon. With the royal delegation retreating now through the East Gate and on toward Jerusalem, the market place filled again with concerned residents as they struggled to assist several people who lay wounded around the tipped and broken meeting table. It soon became clear that in the struggle and confusion that had ensued in the heart of our city, several people had been caught in the stampede of the crowd and seriously hurt. Shock and additional anger erupted when it was discovered that Tabitha's husband was one who had been caught in the crowd of rampaging defenders. Although a man of peace, he, like so many others, had added his blood to the dusted cobblestones of my troubled existence. Elian had been trampled to death!

Chapter 3

Bazar in Joppa 1893 by Bishop John H. Vincent; Rev. James W. Lee

The Strange Visitors

With the death of her husband, Tabitha was faced with tragic loss and the crushing responsibility of making her own way forward in life as a widow and a local merchant. Taking over sole proprietorship of her husband's textile business did not leave much time for extended grieving on Tabitha's part. With the local commerce expanding and greater needs developing among the disadvantaged and poor, Tabitha soon found herself flourishing as business woman and benefactor.

It was to be in the capacity of merchant and seller that she would first hear the tidings of good news concerning the Messiah.

Busying herself with the work of market place sales and commerce, she had been fully engaged in the activities of the day. From her simply-made display of small wooden tables, fine fabrics and handmade garments she greeted travelers, merchants and locals who were packing into the small Joppa village center on that warm spring morning. Tabitha was faithfully engaging the many visitors who inquired of her work. With arms full of colorful textiles she carefully explained the techniques used in manufacturing these materials as well as the sewing and stitching maneuvers she used to assemble the stunning garments that were for sale. As many potential buyers made their way along the main pathway of the market, Tabitha had noticed a number of visitors from Jerusalem and Galilee. She had made it her business to observe the clothing styles and fashions of those who traveled through the area and without error could usually identify the cities and homelands from which her potential customers had come.

On this particular day it seemed an unusual number of her fellow countrymen had arrived from east of the foothills. Rather than just merchants and business people, there were many families with children and couples making their way into Joppa. From the collection of bags and satchels, it appeared to Tabatha, that many were on more permanent journeys to the coast than what would have been usual for spring travel in Palestine. Immediately her mind sprang to life with possibilities. Perhaps the Romans were flexing their military muscle and causing inhabitants to move or even flee the area? Or, could it be that the zealots had stirred up contention and brought down calamity on the Holy City and its surrounding populace again? Or, perhaps, the recent crucifixions, that had defiled the land, had forced many to simply leave the area in disgust and aversion. Whatever the reason, it was clear to this woman of keen observation that something had driven many away from the inland valley of Galilee and Jerusalem on a westward migration. As she watched this movement away from house and homeland, her heart was broken at the isolation and struggle that no doubt awaited many of these political and religious orphans that now made their way to Joppa.

The Message Arrives

It was with these possibilities in mind that she inquired of two couples who were taking time to examine several scarves and head coverings at her tables.

"Shalom!" she called to them across one of her fabric covered tables. "I see you have come from the east county. Do you know of things in the Holy City?" she further probed with her words.

"Shalom to you as well, dear sister!" "We have indeed come from the Judean hill country in the north of Jerusalem and things are not well in the city." came the troubled reply.

"In the days since the death and resurrection of Jesus, the Messiah, there has been much confusion, turmoil and persecution," continued one of the men who stood with the other man and two women.

"Many of His followers are being taken captive and jailed for their association with the Prophet and His leaders." the smaller of the two women added with a spark of concern in her eyes.

"It seems for some, that it is best to leave the area and take up residence elsewhere, at least until it can be seen what the Sanhedrin and Roman Procurator will do with those who have chosen to follow this Jesus!" the other man spoke quietly as he softly fingered a blue and white prayer shawl.

Tabitha did not expect to hear these words. Trouble and persecution were not unusual for her people, the Jews, to experience, but talk of a Messiah, who is reported to have been killed and then resurrected was indeed unusual conversation. And from the precise and easy manner in which these four had told their brief story, Tabitha, was strongly inclined to think that these were among the followers of this Jesus. Perhaps they had come directly from the threat of bodily harm themselves and were among those looking to start a new life beyond their homeland.

"Are you here to purchase goods for further travel or does our fair city greet you with possibilities of settlement and work? Tabitha further questioned her visitors as they stood watching the surge of trade taking place all around them.

"We are as yet undecided." came a thoughtful response from the man who seemed to be the leader of the group. "We will simply attempt to find lodging for the time being and later inquire as to the possibilities of work and permanent housing," he finished.

"Do you know where we can find lodgings for several nights in your fair city?" another of the four asked Tabitha directly.

Suddenly, without warning, an overwhelming urgency came over Tabitha's mind. In an instant she knew that she could not let these people go. She felt strongly attracted to their welcoming manner, simple appearance and in particular, their story. It seemed clear in the inner wrestling of Tabitha's spirit that they should not leave without allowing her to find out more about this Jesus, the one they say is the Messiah. It was obvious, in a moment of time from Tabitha's point of view and in a divine moment of inspiration that these people would need to be her honored guests! In fact, if they were willing to do so, she would bring them home, give them needed hospitality and have every detail of their story told to her first hand.

Quickly Tabitha answered the question and then asked one of her own, "There are several good and decent guesthouses that no doubt would be adequate for your needs, but without causing any trouble or imposing on your plans, may I offer my own dwelling for your stay? I would indeed consider it a great pleasure to provide for your housing myself and in doing so I should indeed have more time to enquire about this Messiah of whom you have spoken. Would you be so kind as to stay with me?"

With a few quick glances toward each other and mutual smiles exchanged between them, the two couples nodded their heads in strong approval and agreed to the offer.

"Thank you, dear sister, we are very grateful for your kindness. To be your guests would be a great honor and it will be our greatest delight to speak to you of the Messiah." They spoke with joy and relief to Tabitha as she beckoned them to follow.

In a matter of a few quick minutes they gathered their belongings and prepared to follow Tabitha home for the evening.

Chapter 4

Tabitha's Open Heart

Over the weeks that followed, this 'anything but chance' encounter in the market place, brought the story of the Messiah, in all of its detail to Tabitha. While going about her daily routine of hospitality and work in the market, long conversations with these four visitors occupied her time. Each of the four presented many descriptions of the appearance of this Jesus of Nazareth in Galilee and Jerusalem which filled her mind with images and imaginings that she secretly longed to have witnessed personally. As the four visitors joined Tabitha in her daily trips to and from the market place and assisted her in the long hours of buying, selling and good natured negotiating, the Messiah's message of dedication, sacrifice and forgiveness was explained in vivid color and clarity.

As the daily routine continued and the four new friends exchanged conversation and details about their lives, both couples gave graphic detail of being threatened by the Jewish authorities. They talked openly of several occasions where they ended up watching some of their friends being dragged from their houses and beaten by leaders and temple guards opposed to the followers of Jesus. They detailed scenes of men, women and children alike being rounded up and marched off to crudely fashioned jail cells. These were quickly built and filled with those who refused to renounce their allegiance to the newly discovered Messiah, as the regular places of incarceration were far too small and inadequate. In many cases the beatings or threats of such cruelty silenced the new believers and drove them into hiding away from the Temple and Jerusalem itself. It was this new surge of hatred and the threat of jail, they explained to Tabitha, that had prompted them to leave Jerusalem and Judea behind and seek temporary shelter in Joppa.

Tabitha's heart broke at the stories of persecution and cruelty and yet surged with wonder sparkling with new faith as the descriptions of the Messiah's brutal crucifixion and wondrous resurrection were sown in her already hungry soul and spirit. The glorious experience of the coming of the promised Holy Spirit at the Feast of Pentecost, the resulting revival fervor, the growth of the believing community AND the persecution that followed were all shared from the vantage point of firsthand experience and involvement.

Each time additional details were discussed and her many questions were answered, Tabitha, became drawn closer to this Jesus of Galilee. More and more she became convinced that these accounts were true and that this Jesus, was indeed the promised Messiah of Israel. Having grown up under the shadow of the tugging and pulling of expectancy on one hand and utter disappointment on the other hand concerning Israel's needed deliverer, Tabitha easily understood the importance of this current development. The daily conversations while working, sharing and talking over meals, clarifying accounts while resting in the evenings after many a long day of work, brought this faithful woman of Joppa to a critical point of decision. It seemed that she could do nothing less than become a follower of this Messiah herself and join in His new way of living.

And so it was, on a quiet and private evening with her visitors and new friends, she began her personal conversion and discovery of the Messiah for herself. The air was warm and dry from the fire that burned slowly at the edge of the entrance to the eating chamber of her small dwelling. Occasionally spirals of thin smoke drifted up and out the doorway. The upper level sleeping quarters were hidden by an overhead covering of thin wooden beams, tightly packed straw and thatch hidden behind several long stretches of woven tapestry. This low overhead canopy fluttered gently in the occasional drift of wind that came from the adjacent cooking area and spread through the small dining area. Pillows and small cushions were scattered neatly along two walls and around the low table that served as the room's centerpiece. This wood and twine assemblage was designed to hold small bowls of fresh baked bread, dried fruit and meat and selections of nuts and goat cheese for any guests who found themselves reclining at its side.

She and her guests lay comfortably among the pillows, while colorful fabric wall hangings behind them seemed to funnel the conversation toward the center of the room. The earthy feel of the room and its close quarters provided an almost sacred atmosphere for the exchange of words that followed. It was here while lounging at the evening meal that Tabitha humbly enquired of her visitors as to the means of becoming a follower of Jesus.

"I am thrilled by the reports of the risen Messiah that you have brought to me", Tabitha offered to her guests as they talked. "Over these past days my heart has been much preoccupied with the news that you have brought my way. It seems as if this Messiah has already captured my attention and now it seems nothing is left but for me to become a follower of this man, Jesus." she continued. "Please give me instruction as to my part in obeying the words of God that have come from this prophet," she further inquired of her companions.

The man who was most often the spokesman for the four said directly to Tabitha. "It is, as we have experienced for ourselves, a simple matter. One has to but believe in their heart, confess with their mouth as we did in the beginning and you will be saved and then as well you may receive the promised Holy Spirit".

Tabitha did not hesitate. Almost before the last words left the visitor's mouth, Tabitha moved from her cushioned place against the wall and bowed low to the ground at the side of the serving table and slowly lowered her head to the dusty mat covered dirt floor. She was ready to believe! Within the next short moments, the other four gathered in kneeling positions beside the seeking Tabitha and joined her with their own intercessions. Then, as prayer filled the room and tears fell softly, a confession of sin was made and Tabitha, believing with all her heart, was filled and sealed with the Spirit of God, becoming a follower of Jesus, the Messiah.

The Change

Tabitha had always been a generous person and had practiced giving and serving with great fervency and regularity. But, now, with knowledge of her new found faith foremost in her mind and the consistent tangible presence of the Spirit of the

Christ accompanying her daily life, she gave herself even more to generosity and aiding the poor. Soon it was clear that so many in the community needed her services as a seamstress and so her greatest delight became the toil and labor in hand sewing beautiful and striking garments that were given to the needy and poor.

In a short time Tabitha found herself a part of a growing faith community. As word of the death and resurrection of Jesus made its way into the city and the region surrounding it, many came to faith in Jesus joining those who were forced to flee the ongoing persecution in Jerusalem and Galilee. As the community of believers grew and practical needs increased among the new immigrants and other converts, Tabitha's gifting and talent began playing an increased role of importance. It was not long before her exquisite work became known throughout the entire Christian church of Joppa. As the believers met in their homes and places of business to pray, worship and learn together, assessment of needs and concerns were always noted and Tabitha and her volunteer helpers sprang into action to see to it that no one with legitimate clothing needs went without. In this effort, Tabitha relished the opportunity to serve and assist and thrilled at the chance to be used by her Savior to bind up the broken hearted and further the spread of the good news of Jesus Christ.

Chapter 5

Traditional site of Tabitha's house; 1893 – by Bishop John H. Vincent; Rev. James W. Lee

Stricken

So it was, that during one of her outings to help the poor, Tabitha experienced the first signs that her health was beginning to be compromised in some way. Making her way along very familiar territory, which had never provided any resistance to her movement and energy, she noticed an increased difficulty in her ability to breathe. Tightness in her lungs and breasts began stifling her ability to breathe deeply and move freely. On this particular day she had made plans to visit a young mother with three small children whose husband and father was missing after having been taken in for questioning concerning his new Christian faith.

Finding her way through the narrow and tangled streets of Joppa, and out to the east of town, Tabitha entered the scattered array of tents and make-shift shelters that housed many of the refugees coming over the mountains from Jerusalem and Galilee. Those who had friends or family in the city made their way in and found lodging there. However, those without personal connections were forced to set up camp and live on the outskirts of the city limits until work could be found, friendships could be fostered with the local people or arrangements could be made to travel further to the north toward Caesarea or perhaps south toward Gaza.

Tabitha had made this trip many times without any trouble. Making her way along the few cobble stoned main streets and the many dusty alleyways and back ways she had regularly brought clothing to many believers and unbelievers alike who found themselves trapped for a time in this place of desert transition. Though it was a route of many miles to leave the city and return, she had done so with a consistent spring in her step and ever present joy in her heart. This trip, however was proving to be a more troublesome journey. Once she was able to leave the numerous clusters of mud and brick houses with their thin and contracted passageways, she found that her breathing was becoming labored and painful. Thinking that perhaps she was simply more tired than usual she did not think much about it, except to stop periodically and rest.

During the whole of her benevolent trip, over and over she was forced to stop, rest, catch her breath and nurse the pain of her breathing. Finally, meeting the abandoned mother and her children under the tattered edges of a large canopy of fabric and rope tied securely to its sharp grounded spikes, Tabitha feebly distributed her precious cargo of clothing to welcoming hands and smiling faces. Many layers of cloth material stretched over carefully placed poles had made for adequate protection from the sun and the wind and so provided this immigrant family with a temporary home. It did not, however, offer the slightest relief for the messenger, Tabitha, as continued bouts with pain, breathing pressure and labored movement told her that something was wrong. Something was very wrong! Now, however, with nothing to be done at the moment to relieve her discomfort, she slowly, with painstaking effort, made her way back into the city, back to her own dwelling and back to her own sick bed. This 'something' had taken her completely by surprise. She had noticed no earlier signs of difficulty and now was left puzzled over why she was feeling so very bad and that so suddenly!

The following days were no better. Each morning she would awaken with a fresh hope in her heart as to the opportunities that the day held for her service, only to find that within hours of her rising, she lost almost all available strength. She could do little but sit quietly by the fire, at home, receiving concerned friends and visitors who had come calling to assist and comfort her in her misery.

Soon the days turned into weeks but with no signs of improvement. Christian friends came regularly to pray with Tabitha and help distribute the garments she continued to make, albeit with greater and greater difficulty. As the weeks developed into months, the prolonged disabled condition she faced brought her needlework to a standstill and the production of her beautiful clothing to an end. The loss of such genuine articles of love and compassion brought a heightened air of concern to the faith community as Tabitha slowly withdrew and relegated herself to what she was sure were her final days. Watched and cared for constantly by helpful and considerate woman from the Joppa church, Tabitha grew weaker and weaker until her death was imminent. As a city I grieved! As a community of close knit people we all grieved. Losing such a one would only add to the sorrow we had learned to embrace over the years.

Chapter 6

Lyyda 1893 – by Bishop John H. Vincent; Rev. James W. Lee

A Distant Hope

Peter looked squarely into the man's eyes. It was clear that he had come to the meeting with expectancy and faith, this was obvious, in Peter's mind, from the sparkle and intensity of his gaze that had captured Peter's attention immediately. Sitting with several family members who had brought him, the man waited patiently, listening intently as the Apostle described to the small group of believers the works of the Holy Spirit that were happening in and around Judea.

The Apostle Peter's arrival in Lydda had caused no small stir and interest. The faith community had gathered in full force to receive him and insisted that while he was there he should bring reports from the saints in others cities and villages. As well, there was great interest in the instruction and teaching that all of the apostles had been bringing to the churches in Judea and Galilee.

For some time now the church leaders had been forced into hiding for fear of the Jewish leaders and their savage commitment to eradicate this new expression of faith by persecution and imprisonment of its' leaders. So with the arrival of Peter, the rumors of peace and stability were being confirmed! Excitement and curiosity punctuated the atmosphere of the meeting as the entire congregation was told of the dramatic conversion of one Saul of Tarsus. This Saul, had single handedly brought fear and terror upon all the believers as he systematically attempted to carry out the instructions of the Jewish Sanhedrin. He had set his heart to destroy the church by arresting any of the so called 'followers of Jesus' that he could find. Although this Saul had not visited the village of Lydda, his activities in Jerusalem and its general vicinity had been reported to the church and many expected that one day soon he would come visiting them with vengeance and hatred as his calling card.

So it was that the awe and wonder among the Lydda faith community was deep and intense. The idea of openness to worship the Messiah and freedom to witness and share their faith energized the Lyddian church. The Apostle Peter was showered with hospitality and asked to meet with the saints daily for prayer, teaching and fellowship. It was in this setting that Peter had first met the man, Aeneas. In earlier conversations it had been learned that Aeneas had been crippled and paralyzed for some eight years and, given the severity of the condition, had been bedridden for all of that time. Now, however, with the arrival of Peter, he could not be kept away from the meetings of the saints. Thus, his family had brought him faithfully to the gatherings to hear the extraordinary things that God was doing in Israel.

Peter, was still looking piercingly into the man's eyes as he stood in front of the gathering of believers, recounting the miracles of healing and conversions that the church was experiencing in almost every corner of the Judea and Galilee. It was mid-story and mid-sentence that the apostle stopped his discourse and spoke directly to the crippled man.

"Aeneas, Jesus Christ heals you. Now, rise to your feet and make your bed!" he spoke loudly to the whole group, but declared to Aeneas with his hand held toward him.

Aeneas looked as if he had expected to receive something from the Apostle. His face was radiant and it seemed that his entire body was leaning toward Peter in anticipation. As the words of healing settled over his hearing, an urgency filled his countenance and he quickly reached outward to brace himself against the dirt floor beneath him. As he did so, an invisible energy appeared to surge and rush into his arms, then move methodically down through each hip and into both of this legs. With a sudden twist and slide against his tattered bed of cloth and matting, Aeneas pulled his weight to his knees and then with one final burst of strength stood to his feet.

Immediately the entire gathering erupted into wild cheers and praise. Those closest to him, who were his family and friends, rushed to his side with jubilant hugs and embraces. Aeneas was completely healed, standing by his own strength with tears of joy streaming and glistening as they trickled down his face. As the celebration continued, Aeneas moved through the crowd giving and receiving embraces and handshakes and spryly bouncing on his two new legs and feet. The visit of this Apostle from Jerusalem had not only brought a good report of God's activity among his people Israel, it had demonstrated the clear power of the Spirit and fueled the faith of the church to bring the gospel to their city.

At this incredible turn of events, the believers were anxious to spread the news to their friends, families and neighbors. Before many days, salvation had made its way into the heart of the city and the church added to its numbers the many who were being saved and restored to health and wholeness.

Chapter 7

The Strange Request

The crowd of mourners grew ever larger as word spread through the church that Tabitha was dying. Each hour now brought more and more grief to the believers as they paid their respects to the dying saint and collected numerous samples of her fine craftsmanship and laid them at the side of her meek and plainly decorated bed. Tabitha was gathering her final labored breathes, nearing the end and barely conscience of the proceedings that were taking place all around her. One by one the believers and supporters left her bedside to sit in the small courtyard near the front of her small house and cry and wail with the grief that hung in the air throughout the entire dwelling complex.

As Tabitha's final breath drifted away and her lifeless body settled into its ridged state of death's stillness, several of her closest friends, women who had assisted her in her work and in her dying days, began the ritual process of cleansing. These dedicated women washed and perfumed her body and combed and plaited her hair, all the while crying and moaning aloud over their loss. As the sound of the wails and moans drifted to the others in the house and courtyard, the finality of her death became clear to all, serving only to thicken the atmosphere of anguish that clouded the minds of the many believers who still lingered.

Once the final washing was completed and spices and perfume were gently rubbed on Tabitha's slowly cooling skin, she was dressed in a simple white robe and wrapped loosely with some of the precious colorful fabric that had been her greatest delight. At this completed stage of the preparation, her small wrapped frame was gently lifted by several of the men, who had stood guard waiting for their wives and sisters, and carried slowly and solemnly upstairs. There it was placed on thin cushions and pillows in the center of the private room where Tabitha had spent many an hour sewing and creating her magnificent treasures. Surrounded by the beautiful specimens of her talent and creativity, Tabitha's cold body lay lifeless and still.

Meanwhile, in the corner of the lower level eating area, an animated conversation had been taking place between several woman and two men. In the waning moments of Tabitha's life, a disciple had arrived from Lyyda with fantastic reports of supernatural occurrences taking place at the hands of a man named Peter. This Peter, it was explained, was an apostolic leader from the Jerusalem church, who had traveled to Lyyda to bring news and teaching to the saints and in the process, was seen working miracles. All reports were pointing to a great spiritual revival settling into the area in and around the cities of Lyyda and Sharon and this was being accented by great miracles! Before the visiting disciple could finish his report, a consensus of several of the local leaders of the church had been made. It was decided that messengers should be sent immediately to Lyyda to inquire of this Peter. Could it be, that perhaps with a visit from this Man of God, the loss of their dear Tabitha could be reversed?

The two messenger disciples left immediately on their half day journey for Lyyda to insist that Peter come to Joppa and attend to the matter of Tabitha's premature death.

The Messengers to Peter

Activity in Lyyda, among the believers, continued with a high level of expectancy and faith. The Apostle Peter joined numerous house groups and small gatherings of disciples to preach and teach and pray for the sick. As the Holy Spirit confirmed his words with marvelous signs, the whole of the community began to awaken to the message of the Messiah. As the number of disciples increased, the news of the gospel and the display of the power of God expanded through their daily contacts with neighbors, friends and family. Even visitors and travelers could be seen conversing and listening to the reports that were filtering through the marketplaces, businesses and daily routines of the city.

It was mid-morning at one such believer gathering that Peter was met with the urgent request to come to Joppa. A morning meeting had just concluded and Peter, along with several of the local church leaders, were resting casually at a low serving table, while fresh provisions of bread and fruit were being sampled by those in the room. As the leaders exchanged conversation and discussed many of the current events taking place in Israel, a noise of commotion suddenly could be heard coming from outside. As the clamor intensified it became clear that two men were in dire need to see Peter; and from the upheaval being created just outside the front entry, they were not to be denied an immediate audience with the apostle. Peter, laying alongside the table, came to an upright sitting position and beckoned to those at the doorway to bring the two men into the room.

The two disciples from Joppa quickly made their way into the small room and found two open places at the side of the table where Peter and several other men were lounging.

"Greetings Brothers! Peace be upon you, in the name of our Lord Jesus!" Peter said after several moments of settling were given the two men. "What brings you to Lyyda with such urgency?", he continued.

"We have come from the believers in Joppa and carry an urgent message and request," one of the two men hurriedly stated to Peter. "A very dear and beloved sister, Tabitha by name, who is well known for her exquisite seamstress work and service to the church and the community has died and thus we bring a pressing request from the church leaders in the city, that you come to Joppa immediately and pray for her!", the nearly exhausted man finished.

With the mention of Tabitha's name, a sudden rush of emotion and concern was sent rippling through the crowd that had pressed into and around the room with the two strangers' arrival. Tabitha and her work were well known even in Lyyda, and the announcement of her death had brought an immediate reaction of grief and sadness to those present. As the whispers of concern and anguish began to subside, the other of the two visitors spoke with an imperative appeal.

"It is our sincere hope that you will return with us at once, seeing it is noon and that the day is already half spent," he finished abruptly.

Seeing the compelling anxiousness of the two visitors, Peter stood to his feet and signaled to his other traveling companions that they should leave at once. Immediately, other disciples gathered meager provisions to be wrapped and packed for the trip to assist Peter, his companions and the two messengers from Joppa. With half of the day now gone, the 5 or 6 hour walk would bring them to Joppa just before dusk and just before the city would begin closing its gates for the night. It was imperative that they get started quickly and make the 15 mile, gently downhill journey toward the Great Sea and the busy port of Joppa as soon as possible.

Chapter 8

Traditional site of Peter's house 1893 by Bishop John H. Vincent; Rev. James W. Lee

Peter Comes to Joppa

The air was still, silent and motionless in the upper room where Tabitha's body lay alone among the tapestry of color and pigment that made up the piles of fabric and material pieces that surrounded her. No one dared enter this quiet place for fear of being overcome with the sorrow of the this loss. Below in the other rooms of the house and still in the outer courtyard of Tabitha's humble home, soft wails of tearful mourning could be heard. The loss of this faithful saint and servant had shaken the believing community and brought sorrow and disappointment to the public in general. In the hours since her death, the whole of my beloved Joppa, it seemed, was laboring under a cloud of misery and pain at the loss of this woman. In the collective mind of the people of Joppa and those Christians in the faith community, her loss had dealt a serious blow to the spirit of generosity that she had made famous in the city. Now, the remote sense of hope or expectancy was hidden far away from the crowds, in the hearts of those few who had dared to send disciples to Lyyda in order to summon Peter. And the longer he delayed the more distant was their hope.

With the sun starting to set over the western edge of the Mediterranean Sea, the city of Joppa was beginning its daily ritual of being secured from the dangers of the night. Bright rays of yellow orange now began to streak eastward over the city and out toward the low hills that spread toward Lyyda and Jerusalem. With systematic procedure, my faithful citizens, approached each giant gate that served to welcome the world through its northerly, southerly and easterly entrances and began the slow process of closure. Large timbers were readied at each location, to eventually be slid into huge iron clamps on the back of each paneled door to hold the gates closed from the inside. As was the custom throughout Palestine, once these gates where closed no one could enter until the following morning. If a party failed to enter the city in the prescribed time, they would be forced to spend the night on their own just outside the barrier walls of the city. It was through one of these easterly gates that Peter, the two messengers and a small group of other traveling companions made their way into Joppa. Traveling from the east, down the gently sloping road into the eastern most limits of the city, visitors would be captivated by the view to the west. The piercing rays of the setting sunlight darting and dancing over the glistening and sparkling surface of the sea seized the attention of all who passed this way into Joppa. With this kind of sunset in full motion, Peter and his traveling companions set their sights on such beauty as they entered the city at just the right time before the sun disappeared in the west.

The Tearful Welcome

With the two disciple messengers leading the way, Peter and his companions were taken without delay to the house of Tabitha. As they made their way further off the main road from the eastern gate and wound their way through the narrow streets and alleyways which led to Tabitha's dwelling, faint high pitched sounds of distress could be heard. Distant echoes of tearful wailing recoiling off the soiled brick and block walls of the many shops and houses greeted the apostolic team as it arrived. Groups of people were still gathered in small huddled circles throughout the courtyard and the home of Tabitha, all of them consumed with grief and mourning.

Peter's arrival brought a flurry of conversation and attention from the all of these who were still waiting. This development had not been expected by the still lingering mourners. It was clear to the Apostle that this woman was indeed cherished by the believers of Joppa, and in fact respected by all, from the number of people who remained at the place of Tabitha's passing. The depth of their sorrow and emotional pain spoke of their love and devotion to such a one as Tabitha. In particular, several of the widows in the church, who had collected many of Tabitha's specimens of sewing excellence, were still present, leaning upon each other for support and strength. These honored women were clustered in the upper level of the house near the room where the body lay silently. Each of them held against their breasts beautifully stitched robes, tunics, prayer shawls, head coverings, and scarves which they thrust out toward Peter as he approached. Peter, the Apostle, had silently been led through the maze of mourners, into the house and to the small staircase that led to the upper level. As he made his way slowly up the stairs from the ground level of the house, he was greeted with thrusting arms and hands holding scores of garments made by Tabitha. Tears of sorrow mixed with cautionary joy greeted him as he came to a full stop looking down at the kaleidoscope of color and texture that now pressed toward him on every side. Just beyond the outstretched arms of layered clothing and over the head of several of these widows, Peter could see the ridged and unmoving form of Tabitha's body. It had now been almost a full day since her final breath and the dispatch of the messengers to Lyyda to bring Peter here.

Chapter 9

Tabitha Rises

Given the loss of time, the Apostle now moved with clear and direct purpose. Gently but firmly Peter sent the mourners out of the room and away from the immediate area of the lifeless body. One by one each widow filed down the stairs toward the others who still waited below, some with sighs and others with quiet lament. In seeing that Peter remained purposely in the upper level and alone in the room with Tabitha's cold body, a stillness of anticipation gradually spread over the whole of the group. In their anguish and distress they were not sure what to expect of this new development. Those who had sent for Peter could only hope for the best. Those who were still mourning and unaware of the Apostle's reason for coming could only guess as to what he might be intending to do.

Now with the room empty, Peter turned to the motionless form of Tabitha and knelt down beside her. For several minutes on both knees and with intense words and cries, the Apostle prayed and petitioned the God of Heaven. Then, shifting slightly and turning to his right toward the body of Tabitha, he spoke.

"Tabitha, get up!" he spoke strongly and in the direction of her head and face.

For a very short moment nothing seemed to happen. The air in the room remained still and heavy. A very weak sound of muffled voices from the house's lower level was all that could be heard as it drifted through the doorway behind Peter. Then, as suddenly as Peter had spoken his command, a flush of rosy tint flickered in the neck and cheeks of the silent and tranquil Tabitha! Spreading instantly over her brow, the warm glow of blushing skin replaced the grayness! A soft rush of air passed over her lips and Tabitha's eyes opened wide, and as her gaze focused, she looked directly at Peter. It was as if she already knew why he was kneeling beside her. Now that strength was already pouring through her body again, without notice she sat upright, smiled broadly and looked expectantly toward Peter. Peter, who had watched her stir to life was now standing alongside the sitting Tabitha. From the full height of his tall rugged frame, he then reached downward securing her small delicate hand and lifted her to her feet.

In the lower lever, conversation was being held to a minimum by some invisible force. A strange mixture of sorrow and hopefulness possessed the still waiting friends. Tabitha's closest friends, widows all, especially were affected by the uncanny atmosphere that dominated the house and its inhabitants. It had not been long since the Apostle Peter had firmly sent them all out of the room above and down the stairs; and although nothing was being voiced among them, many were becoming a bit uneasy with the lack of movement and sound in the upper chambers of the dwelling.

It was with this uneasiness beginning to weigh heavy on their minds that they heard the first sounds from the room above them. It was the voice of a man, the Apostle in fact, calling down to them.

"Brothers and sisters!" Peter called down to them over the low railing that protected the upper passage from the rest of the house. "Tabitha lives!" he continued with force and volume.
"Come and see the power and grace of the Messiah at work!" he finished while gently bringing Tabitha out of the room onto the upper passageway to the top of the stairs.

The reaction was instantaneous! Loud sudden exclamations of disbelief and wonder erupted from almost every quarter of the crowd below. Shrieks of joy, excitement and awe bubbled up and infected the whole atmosphere of the place. As the words, 'Tabitha lives!' penetrated the diminishing hold of sorrow in the air and the few people closest to the stairway caught the first glimpses of Tabitha's erect frame and smiling face, there was a rush of bodies up the stairs and into the arms of Tabitha. A slight shaking of building and ground greeted the multitude in the lower living area and outer courtyard as the thundering mass of sympathizers pounded the wooden framed steps up to where Tabitha was looking down. Quickly they surrounded her and swept her up in their arms and held her affectionately. Tears of joy and excitement, along with kisses of friendship and welcome, greeted Tabitha as she was led down the stairs into the living area below.

The City of Joppa is Shaken

News of such a miracle as this could not be held back. Although many of the believers remained in Tabitha's home to greet and serve their friend, many others immediately left to tell the story of their experience. Spreading throughout the city, the word of Tabitha's resurrection ignited an already smoldering spark into a full blown burn of revival and evangelism. From every section of my beloved Joppa, people traveled to see Tabitha and hear her story first hand for themselves. As well, as the believing community welcomed and embraced my visitors and conversed with the steady flow of people into my hospitable walls, many believed in this Jesus, the Messiah. In this unprecedented flourish of activity, Peter the Apostle found a warm welcome at the home of one of my respected citizens, one Simon, a tanner. It was here, in this location that he continued to receive many visitors and continued sharing the story of the power and forgiveness of the Messiah.

I, Joppa, as a small but busy port city, had witnessed the loss of one of its most famous citizens, fought through a prevailing darkness of grief and sorrow at the loss of Tabitha, and then in a flurry of unexpected and divinely appointed activity saw the power of God bring her back to life. In the restoration of this woman and her mission of service which she had so graciously accepted from God, many found entrance into an eternal kingdom and as a result would dwell within my fair ramparts, never be the same again.

The End.

Story Three

Healing At Bethesda

Douglas S. Malott

Healing at Bethesda
Based on John 5:1-15

Prologue:

I am an old man now and my life will soon be coming to a close like so many others. However, but in facing this reality, I can only rejoice in the fact that my latter days have been more glorious than my former days. You see, very early in my life I was, plagued with a serious and mysterious disease. This mysterious disease attacked me without warning. As a young child, I was, one day running and jumping with other children my age, and the next day I was struggling to stand on my feet without pain. As time passed through those early years of childhood, I became unable to walk or even crawl without extreme discomfort and painful distortion.

As a result of this kind of curse and burden, I was left with little ability to move and the constant paralysis in my hips and legs kept me confined to either my bed, my woven reed mat, or a small stool. After many years of this persistent condition, I had all but given up hope of any recovery. I could do nothing but lay beside the Bethesda Pools begging and hoping against hope for some miracle. Then it was, in the middle of this dark existence that I had a chance encounter with Jesus of Nazareth. Completely without warning or expectation I met the Messiah, and in one short conversation my life changed forever. Let me tell you my story!

Chapter One

Becoming a Cripple

I had been born to a good Jewish family near the small village of Anathoth, which lay just to the north of Jerusalem, the Holy city, on the road to Jericho and the southern shores of the Jordan River. A good half days journey on the Jericho road would bring us to the city if needed and often as a small child I would make this short trip with my family. My father was a herdsman and our family had lived in this general area for four generations. Many relatives on both sides of the family made this rural setting their home. It was not until after my paralyzed condition developed and I became a burden to my parents and siblings that I was forced to relocate to the City of Jerusalem.

I was not too young to remember all of the details of the onset of my malady so with what I have been told by my family, I have marked the beginning of this crippling disease to have begun within a few months of my ninth birthday. With those faint memories still lodged in my mind and the additional information provided by family and friends, the first evidence appeared as I was playing as usual with friends in the open field at the side of our house.

Our simple one story home was clustered with several others houses, and as was the custom, all the dwelling entrances opened into a common courtyard. This kind of living arrangement made for very close knit relations among all of the families that occupied this enclosure together. Over to the east of the main courtyard gate was an unoccupied and undeveloped open field that regularly enticed the local children, myself included, to congregate and spend time together. It was here that most days we spent hours devising endless entertainment and play.

On that infamous and dreadful day, a whole group of my friends and I had gathered to embark on many imaginary adventures. And as it turned out, in the process of interacting with several of my closest friends, pretending to valiantly conquer a Roman Guard, I suddenly lost control of my right leg and stumbled to the ground. I remember only vaguely, as a younger child, having some reoccurring weakness in my lower extremities, but it never proved to be anything that really seemed to slow me down. This loss of control and hard fall to the ground was the first time that any potential physical handicap had become obvious. And in those brief moments of free-fall toward the dusty Judean soil, I had not a clue that this would mark the beginning of the end of my mobility and freedom of movement. It would, in fact, become the day that my whole world would come to a complete stand still and I would remain that way for many, many years.

All of my friends, expecting me to gather myself from the dust and rocks and join them in the ongoing make-believe conquest, at first continued with their supposed attack. So, quite unintentionally, I was left on the ground alone writhing in pain for several minutes. It did not take long, however, before several of my companions noticed that I had been left behind and stopped their pursuit to rally around me. What was not clear to them was that I could not gather myself up from the dusty play field. My sudden pain and subsequent shock had forced me to lay on my back, unable to stand for some time.

Gathered around and looking down at me with puzzled looks of dismay and concern, each of my youthful cohorts seemed stunned into inaction. As I remember it, everyone become quite disturbed when they found I was unable to stand and place my full weight on my painful leg and needed their help to get back home. That was the beginning of a slow, cruel process that eventually rendered me unable to stand or walk. It was in fact with much difficulty that I was even able to sit upright on the ground or even on a short stool. Gradually my ability to stand and walk faded from reality and over the months that followed I was relegated to sitting or lying down, unless of course, carried by some strong and able person.

You can imagine the turmoil and struggle this created for my family and in particular my parents. I soon became a daily burden and challenge for each of them and, as the days and months advanced and turned into several years, it became obvious that a change of location was needed. Moving, perhaps closer to the city, seemed the consensus that would best suit the family and me, given my growing paralysis. Being closer to the city with its services and activities would make more sense than to be left isolated and alone in the countryside of the Judean hills. And so it was, with much deliberation and anxiety my growing burden of paralysis eventually forced us to make the move from rural Judea toward the City of Jerusalem.

It was here, in the north of the city, where many other poor and infirm people had been forced to live for many years that we found ourselves settling down. Small clusters of mud and brick houses were beginning to scatter all across a large area of this open area in the valley below the Mount of Olives. From this point of convergence between valley floor and the low northern hills, the Holy City could be seen in full view to the south. And lifting itself just above the height of the city's 60 foot wall, the upper expanse of the Temple of God revealed itself in its full glory. This whole area to the north of the Temple complex and just outside one of the City's north facing gates, would provide cheap housing, give all of us better access to the markets and provide direct access to the Temple complex. It would also, needless to say, make begging and alms seeking much more convenient and lucrative. But the most important reason that this location was selected was the fact that it would also provide much needed access to the fresh water of the cleansing pools that were so critical in helping ease the pain and discomfort of physical disabilities. Among the several cleansing pools that dotted the Jerusalem landscape, it was one such pool, the one called Bethesda, which would become my home away from home. It was there that I would join a growing and pathetic menagerie of displaced humanity trying to make sense of our plight.

Once our family was permanently settled, the routine for me became a ritual of sorts. On a daily basis I would be gathered up by family or friends and brought to the pool's edge, or, in the warm weather seasons of spring and summer, I would simply stay by the pool for days on end, begging, watching the people traffic and several times a day bathing in the cool waters of the pool. My daily soaking in the pools was the most difficult part of the day since it took most of my strength just to drag myself to the pool's edge and actually reach its water. For the largest portion of an average day I was confined to my mat. Even on my best days it took all the strength I could muster to maneuver the short distance over the inlaid stone to arrive at the pools edge and lower myself into the refreshing water.

Chapter Two

Coming to the Pools

The Pool of Bethesda was actually two large rectangular pools attached by a covered walkway made of huge stone pillars and gently curved stone arches overhead. Each of the pools were surrounded by a low colonnade or portico that was also covered by similarly arched rock. Entry could be made from several large open passageways that were located at the four corners and center of the pool complex. Once inside one could move around the edge of the entire pool structure in hopes of finding an unoccupied place to access the water. Steps leading down into the water were located at the corners of each of the eight sides of the pools. Among the pillars or columns on all sides of the two pools, people could be seen as they spent time moving in and out of the waters to perform ritual cleansing or to attempt soaking and washing away any number of physical discomforts. Many, as myself, who were crippled or lame in some fashion, spent much time along the sides of these pools in order to receive alms or gifts from the more well-to-do Hebrews who frequented these rippling waters.

My first visit to the pools is still etched into my memory, as it was to become the first of a lifetime of visits. At that time in my life, I was young enough and small enough to be carried by a family member, so early on that fateful day I was hoisted onto the back of one of my uncles and carried to the Bethesda Pools. Bouncing gently in the grasp of his strong arms, I could only watch the surrounding scenery pass me on the right and on the left as I strained to look out over each of my uncles shoulders. Not knowing what to expect and having so little control of what would transpire, I remained quiet and somber as we made our way up the main north road toward Jerusalem's Sheep Gate.

As a young boy several distinct memories provide the framework of my recollections of that day. Our short 30 minute walk was largely uneventful except for the press of people that were hurriedly making their way toward the city and the pools. I remember thinking to myself that if all of these people were heading toward the same pools as was I, then I would have a difficult time finding room at the water's edge. I was later relieved to discover that most were heading into the city for reasons unknown to me and not to the pools. Also, I remember the smell of fresh moisture in the air as we turned from the main road and made our way down a short incline toward the pool's entrances on their east side. At the time, I wasn't sure what that meant until we moved up to and through the arched tunnel into the pool's surrounding portico. There, the full force of the scent of cool water met me immediately.

Directly in front of us, I could just make out the shimmering surface of the southernmost pool as I craned my neck to peer over my uncle's right shoulder. To the left and right stood the carved rows of stone columns that supported the colonnade ceilings of additional stone. Looking up at the carved stone archways brought both feelings of excitement and dread as the whole complex seemed to dwarf the two of us as we stood taking in the grandeur of the pool's surroundings. Groupings of people, some rich and some poor, could be seen at strategic places all around the pool's edge, most tucked back just into the shade of the surrounding passageway's overhang. Others could be seen and heard in the pool's water attempting to bathe and soak away their pain and their uncleanness.

After a few moments of assessment, my uncle made his turn to the left toward the center passageway that divided the north pool from the south pool. There he spotted an open area in the corner of the southern pool close to one of two sets of descending stairs that made access to the water easier for the infirm and the elderly. It was here that he gently lowered me to the coolness of the stone floor and slowly rolled out a woven mat and blanket for me to use. With the assistance of my uncle's strength and a few of my own quick scoots and pulls, I secured my place on the mat and then simply sat staring out over the view of the pools. This would begin a whole new learning experience as I would now need to discover how to make myself known to potential alms givers as well as rehearse the shortest distance to the pool and its inviting water. The shortest distance possible to the water would help provide the best chance of seeking its soothing properties. Also, being close to the water would give me the best chance at experiencing the miraculous stirring of the water that we all hoped would rid us of our disabled conditions.

You see, the Pools of Bethesda were unique among the many pools in and around the city of Jerusalem. As I soon discovered from the patrons who frequented this pool complex, periodically the waters were visited by an Angel from God, who would, by all accounts, hover over the waters and stir the pools surface with his wings. This stirring of the water by the angelic visitor was said to release the healing virtue of heaven into the water and as the sick and infirm at the pools edge became aware of this miraculous mingling of heaven and earth, they could be healed. That is, of course, if they were able to be some of the first ones into the water during the moments of the water's movement. This, I was told by many, was both a blessing and a curse. It was a blessing for the few who happened to enter the water at the right moment and receive their healing and it was a curse for all the rest of us who were unable to move into the water fast enough or who, due to other pre-occupations and distractions were just unaware of the angel's presence. However, the hope of such healing; the grand expectancy of such divine activity, kept hundreds of us faithfully lingering at the edge of these tantalizing pools of water many years. For me, most of my 38 years of suffering was spent with the vague hope that I could be the one to touch the water stirred by the angel.

Chapter Three

The Water's Stirring

I had on a couple of occasions witnessed this unusual happening, but was always unable to enter the water in time to be healed. There were few days where my strength level was adequate enough to help myself get into the water and thus I had to depend on the help of others to get me there. But of course, no one could remain with me at all times to assure that I was able to enter the pools. And so I was helpless to be able to respond immediately at any moment to the miraculous stirring of the water.

One particular time that stands out in my mind illustrates the extreme joy and the crushing sadness that was a way of life for those of us confined to the water's edge. This particular day, several years before my encounter with Jesus, The Christ, I was attending my regular duties of calling out for alms. I was laying just far enough away from the pool's edge to be out of direct sunlight, which inundated the entire interior of the pool area. On those bright sunny days, the water's reflection of the sun's rays could have a blinding effect on those of us closest to the water. As well, the heat could prove to be almost unbearable in the middle summer months of Tammuz, Ab and Elul. But, even with these inconveniences of bright sun and heat, I would not allow myself to be too far from the water's edge for fear of missing the angel presence, if indeed he should decide to visit our pool.

That particular day had worn on into a hot and uncomfortable afternoon. Activity around the pool seemed to have waned as I looked out across the expanse of water, stone and covered arches. I could see that the hot afternoon had lulled many into either sleep or into retreating further away from the edge of the pool to find more shade and, so, more relief. I was torn in my own heart as I watched because I certainly did not want to move any further away from the water as others had done, but yet the thought of dragging myself over toward the shade of the adjacent wall and its cooling darkness seemed so enticing. It was at this point in my mental struggle, while gazing upward toward the cloudless sky above that it happened; the angel arrived!

In a moment of time a gentle but swirling breeze seemed to swoop down over the tiled roof of the surrounding walkways and hover over the water. This floating twisting wind above the water held steady in the southern most pool which faced south toward the great Temple of God in the Holy City. My first reaction was to close my eyes and enjoy this breeze that would possibly cool the air a bit all around us. But suddenly, I realized that what was happening was confined to this southern pool only and did not appear to be any usual wind or gust of air. Other large areas of the water's surface did not appear to be affected by this new force of wind.

"Could it be an angel?" I thought to myself.

"Is this the Angel of Healing?" my thoughts echoed back to me.

Immediately I stiffly lifted my upper body to an elbow and tried desperately to roll over on my side so as to make it easier to pull myself to the edge of the pool. By this time others in the area had begun to notice this developing phenomenon and were likewise attempting to get themselves into the water. The scene was quite a sad one as scores of tortured and troubled people began straining to pull, drag and inch themselves into the pool, in case this was indeed the angel's appearance. Groans of surprise as well as curses of frustration could be heard echoing in and out of the columned stone. Having rolled over and begun pulling myself toward the edge of the pool, I could see the water being agitated and sending pulsating ripples out in every direction from the far corner of the pool. I could not see any angel, as others had claimed in previous encounters, but the water surely was being moved by some invisible and unearthly power. Whether or not I could actually see an angle did not matter at the moment, I simply wanted nothing more but to do my best to get into the water!

It was then in this labored effort to reach the water that I heard from the far side of the pool piercing shrieks of screaming and yelling. Someone, who I did not know, was in the water shouting at the tops of their lungs with surprise and shock. From the gyrations being seen in the splashing water of the pool it was clear that a once infirm or handicapped person was experiencing some kind of significant physical change. It was at that point that the cause of the commotion became very clear to me: the angelic host **had** appeared; the healing **had been** released into the water by the angel; a needy recipient for the healing virtue **had been found** ...*and it was not me.*

I had again been unable to get to the water in time. I laid still for a few moments with my eyes closed, while the weight of disappointment pressed through me. After a few grieving moments, I gathered my little strength as the gloom of having missed the water's stirring draped over me, like a hot smothering cloth. Activity around me lost its meaning, clarity and focus, diminishing to a muffled vague stillness. All that was left in my hearing now was the remaining laps of water on the pool's side, the distant and fading cries of joy from the now healed person as they moved further from my location, and a faint last wisp of breeze from the whirlwind as it dissipated and disappeared. Again, with many others at the pool's edge, I was forced to hang my head in deep displeasure.

This experience was typical for so many who spent their entire lives around these pools hoping to catch the angel's stirring before anyone else could. I had over the years heard many stories of such failures to enter the water. Only a few recollections included the positive accounts of some who plunged into the water first among the many who tried. With the failure to get to the water in time, I was now included among those who had firsthand experience in such overwhelming grief and disenchantment. I will never forget that day, as it proved to be a mixture of extreme sadness and a strange kind of hope. Hope because although I had not been able to get to the water, someone had and thus they had been healed and so I was still determined to be ready for the next encounter. I did not know at that point that my next encounter would not be with an angel, or agitated water in a pool, but with a person, the Messiah, God's anointed Savior and healer.

Chapter Four

A Glorious Day

     Standing here now on the full strength of healthy feet and legs, carries my mind back to the very time and place of that glorious day. Recounting it is like being there all over again. The day began and developed like all days previous. My pain and immobility left me laying mostly prostrate on my small but adequate mat staring up at the open sky above me. With an occasional turn of my head, I could see that the activity around the pool's edge included all of the usual needy and religious people, however this day perhaps things did seem to be somewhat busier than usual. I was not sure why this was the case until I noted that several groups of people were gathered under the center archway as if anticipating the arrival of someone or something important. This was not completely unusual since periodic visits by dignitaries, royalty, governing priests and others were organized by the city officials. In those cases, however, we who were crippled or poor and begging, were herded back into the shadows of the surrounding colonnades, mostly out of view, so as to not interrupt or embarrass the special visitors.

     On this particular day numerous groups of people and priest, from the Temple milled around the pool's edge waiting, but no effort was made to move or hid the presence of the infirm and sickly that made the pool their home. Given this reprieve, I simply attempted to rest and be ready for the day's possibilities. My resting was eventually interrupted by the echoing sound of shuffling and tapping sandal leather against the portico's stone floor. My first reaction was to hide my face and lay as still as possible, hoping that there was not a sudden change of heart and an attempt underway to move me. Next, after realizing I would be moved, my mind jumped quickly to the possibilities of receiving a generous gift; so, naturally, almost without thinking, I attempted to roll onto my side and to reach for my battered, chipped and dirty hollowed-out gourd so that I would be ready to accept any spare coins that could come my way.

Looking up I was surprised at what greeted my eyes. There were no begrudging clients attempting to satisfy their guilt by handing down to me some of their spare change. Instead of outstretched arms with clinched fists holding coins, I saw the gentle smile and sparkling eyes of a man in a long robe standing over me. This man had no coins to offer that I could see from my awkward position beneath him. As he bent over slightly toward me, his long tangled brown hair fell softly forward from his shoulders. This framed his face and highlighted his intense look of concern for what he saw helplessly laying in front of him. As I struggled to readjust my focus and posture for this new development, I could do nothing meaningful except look longingly into his interested face. It was then that the inquiring man spoke directly to me.

"Do you want to get well?" He said to me quietly as if I was the only one in the entire pool area.

The question took me by surprise! I had not expected a conversation with any curious visitors. And the nature of his inquiry sent puzzling waves of shock through my head. Never before had my day included concerned people asking me if I wanted to get well! Did I want to get well? Indeed I wanted to get well, but each time I attempted to do so by getting into the water of the pool, I would fail and having no one to help me only compounded my inability. Of course I want to get well, I thought again to myself!

"Sir," I finally replied in desperation, "I don't have a man to put me into the pool when the water is stirred up! While I'm coming to the pool's edge, someone else, in another location along the water, goes down ahead of me, and they are the ones that are healed," I finished slowly.

I was not sure at that point what I expected to hear in return. I had simply given him the answer to His question. Anyone accustomed to the activity around these pools would know that only a few are ever healed when the water is stirred, while most who reside here are not! But in giving my answer, never in my wildest dreams did I think His response would be one of healing!

"Sir, get up," the man spoke directly to me again, "pick up your mat and walk!" He finished with an abrupt but emphatic expression of authority.

As the words, *'pick up your bed and walk'*, came strikingly into my thinking, a strange sensation of energy and vitality began moving through my lower body, from my feet, up through my legs and into my hip and waist area. Tingling and a slight quiver traveled up my limbs with this energy surge. A wave of coolness spread up my feet and legs as circulation and nerve stimulation punctuated the movement of the tingling. What seemed like a slow-motion period of some time in my brain was actually only a matter of a few brief minutes. This energy building inside propelled me first into a sitting position and then to my knees and then to the full height of a normal standing position. Bubbling sensations of joy and light headedness quickly swept over me. I was standing on my own two feet and flexing my legs and hips in a daze of wonder. Abruptly, I remembered all of the words He had commanded me. Not only had he commanded me to walk but He had also told me to *'pick up your bed'*. So, as quickly as I had stood to my feet, I bent, knelt to the ground and frantically rolled and folded my bedding and scooped it all up into my arms, while at the same time prepared to make the effort to take my first few steps out of 38 years of misery.

Chapter Five

The Confrontation

I had not taken more than a dozen steps before I was halted by several Jewish leaders who had been following this prophet into the Bethesda Pool area. Their look of sternness brought me to a complete stop under the colonnade covering to the west of the southern pool. As I looked at their faces and priestly robes, I realized that these were the same individuals who had been gathering earlier along the pool's center passageway. Suddenly, it became clear to me; these men had come purposely to examine the activities of the man in the long robe who had spoken to me earlier. And what of that man! Looking quickly around, I could see that he had somehow slipped through the crowd and away from the pools. He was nowhere to be seen!

"This is the Sabbath!" these priestly subjects called out for all in the pool complex to hear.

"It is illegal for you to pick up your mat on this holy day!" they continued harshly.

Indeed it was the Sabbath and although I would have never purposely violated the law, this seemed to me to be a righteous exception to the rule. I had been grievously crippled for some 38 years and now at the words of one man, this Jesus of

Nazareth, I had been completely healed. Picking up my bed roll and leaving the scene of my past illness and meager life seemed only appropriate under the circumstances.

Embarrassed and startled, I responded with the only explanation that made sense to me at the moment.

"The man who made me well told me to pick up my mat and walk." I said questioningly.

"Who is this man who told you to pick up your mat and walk?" they retorted with quick and decisive anger.

I did not know who the man was, or why he had approached me among so many that were needy that day. And indeed, I would not find out His true identity until later in the day. Frightened by their angry questioning I began again to look around the pool area in one last attempt to find this miracle man. But as I did so, it only confirmed that he had gone. The Jewish leaders, following my gaze and searching eyes, also looked out over the scene in hopes of finding this man, but they too found that he was gone. As I watched their unsuccessful gazing about and noted the miracle man's uncanny absence, I wondered if it had not been planned. His appearance at my side, His sudden command to walk and then His departure was so suddenly accomplished that I was certain it had to have been planned or else we should have been able to see Him in the crowd that would have naturally gathered.

Slowly, the group of Jewish leaders disbanded their circle around me and went their way. With the atmosphere clearing of their suspicion and accusations I again felt the rush of joy and exhilaration at having my health restored to me. Out loud I questioned my own soul as to what should come next.

"Now what would I do? Where should I go?" I questioned myself.

"Did I have time to find my family? Should I stay and encourage the others who were still waiting at the water's edge? What should be my first course of action?" I mumbled to myself again out loud.

"Should I try to find this prophet, this miracle worker and thereby discover His true identity? I continued in my whispered self-argument.

For several minutes I pondered my decision and my new found freedom. Indeed, what was overwhelming in my bantering conversation was the realization that if I so desired, I could now **do it all**. As my mind weighed and wrestled the best of all my choices, one final thought settled on my mind. It occurred to me that the most important place to be at this point in my deliberations was as near the Temple of God as possible. It would be there that I would be able to offer prayers of thanksgiving and gratitude to the God of Israel for His incredible mercy and my new found liberty.

Thus, I made my way out of the Bethesda Pool compound to the west and made a straight course for the Temple's north side. The walk up the main connecting road as it ascended to the Sheep's gate at the Antonia fortress, was like a dream, I was almost floating as I scuffled alone through the dust and gravel toward the great Temple of God. If this had been any other day but the Sabbath, no doubt several members of my family would have already arrived and been able to celebrate this miracle with me. But, as it was, given Holy Day requirements and duties, they would be forced to arrive later in the day to check up on me as the Sabbath Day began to close. However, their later arrival was the last thing on my mind at the moment; all I could think of now was to get to the Temple before the sun set. Any family, who did eventually come to spend time with me, would have to expend extra energy today to find me, since I would **NOT** be resting by the pools.

Ascending the broad steps from the gate up through the entry point onto the expanse of courtyard of the Temple, only served to increase the emotions of gratitude and joy that now drove me onward. I quickly traversed the outer Gentle Court, entered and skirted the edge of the Court of the Women and finally passed through the arched passageway into the inward Court of the Men. Once inside I found a private area at the east side to give me the best view of the Great Temple of God as it towered just beyond and above the wall that separated the men's court from the Priest's court. I had been prohibited from entering this area for so long because of my previous crippled condition. But now nothing could keep me out! With the sun just now dipping behind the upper precipice of the Temple's roof and shooting out its final burst of yellow-orange rays toward me, I found a sacred spot and quietly knelt to pray. With my former bed roll now unrolled under me as a prayer mat, I covered my head and poured out my heart to the God of Israel, offering heartfelt prayers of thanksgiving. For some time, tears of joy and relief rolled down my cheeks and face as I relished the solitude of my private intercession with the God of Israel.

Chapter Six

Meeting the Miracle Man

After some time of quiet meditation, I became aware that someone else had joined me in prayer. Pulling my head scarf slightly to the side to view my visitor, I was startled to see the miracle man from the Pools of Bethesda crouching down on one knee next to me. Raising my head upward and tilting back on my heels, I was quickly able to see him clearly. Now, unlike my previous encounter, I could see him face to face, without the previous emotion and shock I had experienced at the Pools of Bethesda. Looking fully into his welcoming eyes made me realize who this man really was and the full importance of what he had done for me earlier. This was the man they called Jesus of Nazareth, the one who many felt was the promised messiah. I had heard of him many times and been told many amazing stories of his preaching, ministry and service in and around Jerusalem, but being confined for so many years to my mat in the Bethesda pool compound had prevented me from having any first hand contact with him. And of course those long years of paralysis had prevented me from having any hope of receiving from Him. That is, until earlier in the day when He spoke those glorious words to me, "Get up, pick up your mat and walk!"

I was not sure what the Jewish leaders thought of this man, nor what my friends felt about his life and ministry, but I certainly had every reason to believe that He was called of God and rightly considered to be the Messiah. After a few moments of silence and with the muffled prayers of many others still humming quietly in the background around me, this Jesus reached for my arm, firmly gripping my wrist and then spoke briefly and directly to me.

"See, you are well." He spoke assuredly to me, nodding slightly toward my legs.

I, nodding back to Him in an accenting gesture, heartily confirmed his words and did my best to show my gratitude through the gleaming look of hope on my face. I still struggled to find any words that would adequately convey the sheer ecstasy of joy that coursed through my soul at that moment. The warmth of His countenance, however, served to disarm any awkwardness between us and even though we were very much strangers, something about his accepting approach made me feel like a close friend for those brief moments that he addressed me.

"Be sure that you do not sin anymore! In this way nothing worse will happen to you." He finished, removing his hand from my arm and gently placing it on my shoulder as he stood to leave.

I wanted so badly to talk to this man, to express my gratitude in words not just in feelings, but something in his eyes assured me that he understood my heart and that this passing encounter was better than making a public scene and drawing attention to his presence and activities. With this final conveyance of assurance and loving warning, he moved off to the side and disappeared into the crowd of my fellow praying Jews, who were still filling the courtyard around me with the rhythmic pulsations of their prayers and swaying heads.

Looking out over the busy traffic of robed and scarfed men making their way around the open courtyard, I still bubbled over with excitement over my healing. My spirit was praying but my mind was racing through a whole host of activities that I so wanted to embrace, now that I could walk and run again. Taking in the full scene of dedicated worshippers and the dotted groups of assisting Levitical priests brought me back to the ritualistic reality that surrounded me. These dedicated Levites stood throughout the courtyard ready to offer their assistance to any in need. I told myself that I would first finish my prayers and then I would have time to give my new legs and feet their full freedom to roam and run.

It was then, however, as I attempted to resume my humiliation before the Temple, that I recognized two of these men. These were talking with several others in a small group on the far side of the court from where I was kneeling. Well toward the front stairs that led up to the front porch and pillared entry of the Temple's inner sanctuary, these two men were engaged in conversation while keeping a watchful eye on the busy atmosphere of worship that filled the courtyard. As I watched these two, I remembered where I had seen them before. These were part of the questioning group that had challenged me in the pool compound immediately after I was healed. They were the ones who had taken exception to me carrying my bed on the Sabbath.

As I watched them converse and debate among themselves, I remembered their original inquiry. These had not only ignored my healing and challenged my right to carry my bed on the Sabbath but they had demanded that I identify the one who had worked the miracle of healing. At that time, I had not known who he was, where he had come from or by what authority he could have commanded my healing. But now, with the afternoon events behind me, which had included having had my own second visit from the Man from Galilee, I knew exactly who he was and could see no good reason to keep that fact to myself. In two brief conversations with this Jesus, I had been completely healed and I was now ready to tell whomever needed to know. As I continued gazing over at their familiar faces it only took a few brief minutes of thinking, to decide that it was the right time to tell these men of my discovery.

Now with my new found strength and ability to move I slowly made my way around the cloistered groups of Hebrew men and set a path directly over to this cluster of priestly leaders. After arriving unannounced and standing within talking distance for several moments, I slowly but firmly interrupted their conversation. Politely excusing myself, I stepped slowly between the two men who I had met earlier in the day, facing the one who had made such a self-righteous ruckus earlier. In doing so, I simply waited until he recognized who I was. The one I was facing did not address me directly or offer to exchange any pleasant words, he simply stepped back two steps as he worked hard to purposely put a more safe and protective distance between us. Although he had stepped back, as if to give himself more time and room to look me over, I knew by the look on his face that he recognized me from the earlier pool encounter.

As a few uneasy seconds passed between us and the recognition of who I was become clearer to him (and his friend), I took advantage of their new perspective to speak. With both men looking me over as if needing to decide whether I had permission to make such an approach toward them in the first place, I merely conveyed a matter-of-fact answer to their earlier questions.

"Excuse me Sirs! I am the man from the Pools of Bethesda where you earlier questioned me about carrying my bed on the Sabbath. At that time you had asked me to identify the man who had given me permission to take up my bed and walk on the Lord's Holy Sabbath. At that time I had not known his name." I announced to my startled listeners.

"However, since our earlier afternoon conversation, I have discovered his name. Indeed now I know that this man who worked my miracle of healing at the pool's edge was Jesus of Nazareth. He is the one whom many believe to be the messiah," I stated clearly.

They said nothing in return. Their looks of confusion and disdain along with the unwillingness to respond did not surprise me. The blindness they had exhibited toward my healing earlier in the day told me they were not open to such demonstrations of grace. Their preoccupation with the strict letter of the law also gave me no assurance that they would be receptive to this Jesus of Galilee. Thus, with only silence hanging heavily in the air between us, there was nothing left to do but to turn and walk back into the crowd of worshippers that continued their prayer rituals around me and make my way back across the Court of Men.

I made no effort to look back and see what kind of delayed reaction my announcement may have produced from these two priests as I walked away. And as the distance between us grew and the puzzling looks on their faces were lost in the crowd, the continued silence they purposely maintained, only served to confirm they had no interest in pursuing me for any further information. I had been able to easily determine by the startled and grim looks on their faces when I finished making my announcement, that my information was not a surprise nor was it welcomed. But, given my new lease on life, their rejection did not concern me in the least. I had met the one man that could make the biggest difference in my life and that was enough. I had met Jesus and that one encounter had changed my life forever.

The end.

Story Four

The Leprosy Cure

Douglas S. Malott

The Leprosy Cure

Based on Luke 17:11–19

The Prelude

In the land of Israel, early in the first century of the modern Christian era many significant human stories were played out. One of these stories was of an anonymous leper, who must live his life in relative isolation due to his serious skin condition. Another, the story of the promised Messiah of Israel and His eventual death and resurrection. These two stories, although vastly different in scope and detail, found a point of convergence in the City of Capernaum.

For the leper, a normal day of begging and curiosity turned into a dramatic miracle and a complete change of life. For the Messiah, Jesus of Galilee, a purposeful journey of preaching around the Sea of Galilee and a destined visit to Jerusalem brought Him to Capernaum and a simple exchange of words with a group of desperate lepers. These words served to confirm the authenticity of the Messiah's claims and to completely redirect one very grateful leper into a life of hope and faith. In the pages that follow you will discover a fresh glimpse of what might have been the leper's story, told in his own words.

Douglas S. Malott

Chapter One

An Overwhelming Joy

As the cold refreshing water cascades down over my neck and shoulders, a rush of tears flood into my eyes. I cannot hold back the emotion! The utter and absolute joy I am feeling is overwhelming. Again I reach down to the surface of the lake water, plunging my wooden bucket under the sparkling shimmer of the inviting water. As the water rushes into the lowering bucket's empty space to fill its beckoning cavity, I stoop, watching intently the swirling, cascading water pour into the bucket, and then I lift and pull hard. Up from the shimmering shallows comes another full, tipping and splashing container of water that I hoist and empty again over my head. Down it gushes around my neck and shoulders, drenching my back and chest and leaving me shivering with relief, refreshment and excitement in the bright afternoon sun.

Standing knee deep in the shoreline waters of the Lake of Galilee to simply wash off the dirt and sweat of a hard day's work is still such a new experience of excitement. Such a normal daily event still leaves my heart stunned and dazed with pleasure each time I perform its necessity. The sun's warmth and penetrating heat stir deep profound feelings inside of me that are very hard to explain and the look of the healthy and smooth skin that covers my neck, upper chest, left leg and both forearms brings again unhindered words of praise to God Almighty.

"Indeed, His mercy endures forever!"

You see, my friend, the simple privilege of being employed and able to work has thrilled me again today! Indeed, being able to move about, interact with friends and acquaintances, and actually expose my skin to the elements and the casual gaze of others, makes me feel like a young child with a brand new toy with which to play! There have been many times when I have been giddy with happiness, unable to squelch my laughter. Still, at other times, I can do nothing but just cry out tears of joy, due to my new and glorious freedom.

This has not always been the case, however. My reality and way of life, up until a year ago which was about the time of the previous barley harvest, had been hopeless, dark and foreboding. In fact, I had been an absolute outcast. Rejected and shunned by most of my family and friends and literally all who lived in Samaria, I was hopeless, lost and truly wishing daily that my life could be cut short so that the end of my suffering would come. **You see, I was a Leper.** Doomed to a life of rejection and isolation, I lived among the other vagabond lepers of our nation as a second class citizen. We were simply to be avoided or feared or both.

Then, it happened! In this condition of total despair, a completely unexpected encounter took place. I had a chance meeting with the Man from Nazareth and literally *everything changed*.

Chapter Two

The Fearsome Diagnosis

Let me tell you my Story.

    As a young Samaritan man of 22, I had all of my life ahead of me. All of my dreams and plans were still in my future, all of them yet to come true. I was hoping, that with the right training and apprenticeship I could become a skilled leather craftsman and take a productive place among my own people. As an ancient people, we, the Samaritans, were isolated from the rest of the nation of Israel and disliked immensely by the religious Jews and the cultural elite of their race. This hatred and disdain was due largely to two historical factors; first, we were seen as a mixed race of people; we, they said, were of an impure bloodline. Our original Hebrew bloodline had been mixed with 'gentile' people who were forced to repopulate our land during the Assyrian rule of our nation many centuries earlier. Second, there was still strong generational hard feelings from the original division between the Northern and Southern tribes of Israel, which took place soon after the death of the Great King Solomon.

    This long standing division AND the mixture of unacceptable racial blood made us unfit for Jewish worship and unclean in our standing before God. At least, this was the official religious point of view. Although we were allowed limited access to Jerusalem and the Temple of God, thanks to another great King of Israel, Hezekiah; we were not trusted and for the most part were viewed as second class citizens. In this atmosphere of rejection most Samaritan men constantly fought the inner demons of their lack of clear identity and their hopelessness about the future. With this fog of questioned identity and desperation hanging in the cultural air, success in our culture was idolized and almost worshipped. So, as I watched others my age struggle to be successful, it only motivated me more to make my dreams come true.

And so, it was a fearful and disgusting thing to notice one morning, as I was dressing myself for my daily routine, a discolored area of skin on my upper chest. This skin abnormality was about the size of small coin, slightly grayish in color and beginning to split and discard small flakes of dried dead skin. In the very beginning I tried to wash it clean as often as possible and kept it from being seen by family or friends. I was very familiar with the 'unclean' lepers and their families that begged and roamed aimlessly along our dusty roads seeking any kind of help or handout. These pitiful ones could be seen regularly sitting at a distance around most of our public market places. In their pathetic condition they could be heard calling out for food or money or seen stretching scarred and crippled hands and arms to any who would venture to come close. These people were viewed with a confused blend of revulsion and pity and thus most would scurry away in fear. Some, of course, would cast a coin or a food item or maybe a clothing item their way in hopes of lessening their pain just a little. To consider the possibility of becoming one of them was a horror beyond all imagination.

But, to my dismay, the small aggravated area of skin did not remain small, but instead it slowly, over the months, became larger. It was when a new area of infection developed on my lower arm that I was forced to take action. It was then that I approached my brother and confided in him about my dilemma. Because of the feared mystery surrounding the matter of leprosy and the cultural anathema it created among Samarians and Jews alike, indeed all people, this was taken as a very serious matter. Soon my widowed mother and her brother, one of my uncles, became directly involved in the inspection of my new skin condition. It only took a few close examinations to start the conversation of whether or not I needed to be officially examined by a priest.

The very thought of such a process struck fear and dread in my mind. I had heard many strange and haunting stories of such examinations and the quarantine that was required before a final pronouncement could be made. My family began weighing the need of making such plans to bring me before the priests, which of course, was required by the Law of Moses. Only after a couple of days, with my skin condition worsening was it decided that I must be officially examined. And, of course, since it could not be done in or near our village in the north of Samaria, it would force us to take a long trip to the Holy City of Jerusalem and have private consultation with one of the Levitical Priests on duty in the great Temple of God.

The Priest's examination would result in either a series of weeklong quarantines to make sure the skin disorder would not spread, or if it was determined that the condition was already infectious and spreading, an official pronouncement of 'unclean' would be declared. **This pronouncement would be almost like a death sentence!** It would force an almost unbearable upheaval to my life and thrust me into an existence of isolation for the rest of my days. As the law required, an 'Unclean' pronouncement would automatically require several things to happen. First, my clothes were to be torn and worn in tattered display as a mark of my impurity; next, my hair was to be worn long and loose, I suppose to represent the uncontrolled nature of the infection; then, my mouth was to be covered or veiled whenever the general public was near in an attempt to curb the spread of such infection; also, along with this was the requirement to shout, "Unclean! Unclean!" whenever in public in order to warn people of the infectious condition so they would have advance warning and be able to stay clear of the person infected. And finally, a last requirement was imposed that served to finalized the rejection and isolation; all infected people where to live away from any city or village settlements so as to control the spread of such skin diseases. Thus, diseased or leprous individuals, for the most part were forced to live alone and fend for themselves in small colonies and huddled groupings well off the beaten path of society.

The day of my examination left me emotionally scarred and physically marked for life. Making our way south from Samaria to Jerusalem was a two day journey and both days as we walked and talked, my mind was filled with repeated waves of anxiety and fear. Traveling to Jerusalem and the Temple was an intimidating experience all by itself, without the burden of sickness hanging around ones shoulders. But, with the ever present reminder of my serious skin condition badgering my thinking, the trip was a torturous journey. Even the ominous view of the Holy City, with its ancient walls and tall regal gates did not quell the internal storm raging in my brain. After entering the city from the north side and making our way up to the broad expanse of the outer courtyard of the great Temple of God, I was taken privately along a side wall to a predetermined area under a portion of King Solomon's portico. There selected priests, appointed for such duties, were waiting to examine any concerned individuals. I found a place in line and listened and watched as the many people ahead of me were examined and declared 'clean' or 'unclean'. The atmosphere was rife with emotion and fearful energy. I watched relief drop down over the faces of so many who were told their condition was not infectious and the pronouncement of 'clean' was given to them. But, as well, I heard the occasional scream and wail of fear and grief pierce through the air as the 'unclean' pronouncement was also handed down.

As my turn came and I slowly removed the upper portion of my tunic to allow the priest to have a clear unhindered view of my inflamed and painful skin, I could see the concern increase in the eyes and on the face of the Levite who quietly looked over my severely irritated skin. As his eyes closely examined my aggravated skin, his mannerisms became more subdued and somber. In opposite affect my heart beat quickened and seemed to pound in my chest. At the same time my emotions began their slow sink into sadness as the stillness in the air deepened and the priest's physical motions became ridged and stiff. These, of course, betraying his stilted effort to be neutral and calm.

Saying nothing with his voice but conveying with his body language his fear and a sense of foreboding, he stepped backward slightly and slowly looked down toward the rock tiled floor beneath us. This only served to increase the intensity of my own apprehension. Finally, he lifted his face to gaze directly into my eyes and speak. Although careful and empathetic the words, like tiny daggers thrown into my soul, came pointedly from his pursed lips and stuck one by one into my mind, "My brother, you are unclean!" he said.

Instantly my eyes were filled with burning cascading water. Tears of excruciating fear bubbled over and spilled down both of my cheeks. Weakness suddenly gripped my body like an overpowering wind. My strength and ability to remain standing was now gone. I could do nothing but drop feebly to my knees on the rock pavement beneath me and slowly hang my frail head over my chest. My cloud of terror and horror was only interrupted momentarily by the groans and cries of my family who were standing and now kneeling beside me. For what seemed like several minutes, the hustle and bustle of the Temple's activities was muffled around me.

The outside world, for a brief time did not seem to exist; only my sobbing and groaning and that of my family pressed in around me like a thick blanket. It was only the shrill sound of the priest's pronouncement as he shouted for all to hear, "Unclean, he is Unclean! This man is unclean!" that broke the muffled stillness. As the words rang out I was stunned and shocked again by their sound and left emotionally and physically paralyzed by the weight of their impact. Indeed it was only with the sudden and swift grip of several family members and the prodding of one of the Temple guards that I began to move at all and to make my way out of the Temple complex.

Chapter Three

A Life of Rejection

It was now into a lonely and bitter world that I would travel. The parched and rugged hill county that surrounded the Kishon River valley of Northern Samaria would now become my home and **my prison** for eleven years. As I stumbled and staggered my way out of Jerusalem; held, prodded and at times dragged along the rocky pathways and roads by my brother and uncle, I was still lost in my unbelief and shock. It seemed that a dark nightmarish dream had engulfed me. I wanted to run! I wanted to hide! I wanted to become invisible with my curse. My mind wrestled through the scenes and words that had just confronted me in the Temple. I still could not believe what had just happened to me and yet it had and its reality was now crushing me. Only weeks prior, I had been an energetic young Samarian man with dreams in the making and a life of potential ahead of me, but now I had become a leper and an outcast among my own people. And it would not be until another fateful day at the end of those eleven prison years that my life would have any shape, focus or purpose.

Upon returning to our village, I was required to immediately begin gathering my belongings and making arrangements to leave for the wilderness as soon as it was possible. It would be there that I would be joining others who had discovered they too shared the same fate as I. Although everyone was cordial and gracious, no one wanted to be exposed to such an inexplicable disease, so leaving as soon as I could was the only way to bring a sense of peace back to my village. For the day that it took me to gather my clothing, adequate supplies and several useful tool items, I seemed to be in a constant daze of sorrow. Often, as the hours passed, I would find myself lost in my thoughts and unable to hold back tears as I attempted to go about my business of preparing to leave.

My brother, mother, uncle and numerous other family members and friends made many awkward but sincere attempts at saying good-bye, while trying to stay at a safe distance from my diseased body, which was now covered entirely with purposely tattered clothing. It was clear that leprosy had struck a decisive blow to me as well as the people I loved. But, even so, the only way to deal with the current reality was to leave as quickly as possible and hope that my family could find the courage to venture past their fears and make the effort to stay in contact as I went about my wilderness living.

Once away from the village I soon found that numerous other people with various degrees of infectious skin diseases had gathered in the valley of the Kishon River near the small village Ginae. It was here in makeshift tents, hastily erected lean-tos and small caves that so many similar human outcasts had made their way. From up and down the entire valley these social and cultural rejects came to join ranks and hopefully establish some semblance of a living routine and support network. The atmosphere of hopelessness was a brooding canopy that hung over the entire setting. Here, among these ragged rejects of society, I would be forced to live. It was only after several weeks of depression and the shedding of many tears that I could even begin to resolve myself to the routine of a leper's life.

Over the months and years all of us who were relegated to this isolation and rejection became a living breathing support structure for all who suffered the same debilitating diseases of the skin. All of us, individuals, families, young and old alike, did our best to make ends meet. Some existed by raising small herds of goats or sheep, others by performing some limited farming and some by engaging in very limited trade business. For the most part, we survived by receiving gifts and supplies from our family members who had not rejected us outright, and by regular and consistent begging. After several months of absence from my village, my mother and brother began making regular trips, usually two times per month, to make a brief visit and bring basic supplies and clothing. Never did the visit last long as the fear that somehow the infection growing steadily in my body, and the others around me, might spread to them. Although these visits and supplies were useful, it was the begging that brought the most results and the best source of provisions. Given that fact, all of the men who could manage to be mobile would travel in groups to where ever the most people traffic was available and spend day upon day asking and begging for help.

It was in one of these groups of beggars that I first heard of the man from Nazareth, who many thought to be the Messiah. Family members bringing supplies every so many weeks also brought the reports to us of what was happening in the rest of Samaria and greater Israel. From these visits, reports began to trickle in that a roving, itinerate band of disciples, led by a man named Jesus who hailed from Nazareth and Galilee, was preaching to large crowds and some said, performing great miracles.

Chapter Four

Meeting the Nazarene

On one of our trips toward the City of Capernaum, the conversation among my group of begging lepers eventually turned to the subject of the Messiah. Conversation and debate centered on whether or not this Jesus of Galilee might indeed be the chosen one. Most in the group did not show much interest in this traveling preacher, unless of course, he would be able to help with significant handouts of food, money or clothing. A few in the group offered a slightly more positive view. Their perspective was simply that if the reports of the miracles were indeed true, it might be that we should pray that some of us would receive our own miracle.

This idea was encouraging, although from the way they bantered back and forth in their conversation, it did not seem to me that any of them really believed they might be a recipient of such mercy, let alone actually have their leprosy cured. So, it wasn't long before the subject of the Messiah was dropped and lost in the ever pressing need to approach as many travelers as possible that frequented this main route of commerce. From this point just south of the City of Capernaum and the Lake of Galilee, the road continued southward where Jericho and Jerusalem lay hidden over the horizon. This main thoroughfare of people traffic, moving up and down the valley from north to south, made for consistent opportunities for begging.

This particular day was not proving to be a productive one. The usual crowds of people were not materializing and the longer we waited the more obvious it became that an early return to the colony was the best option. It was not long after our return home that the reason for fewer people on the road became obvious. There was a buzz of excitement in the camp and upon inquiring about this strange atmosphere of enthusiasm and eagerness, we were told that the man from Nazareth had been seen traveling in the area. Apparently he was preaching along the way as he traveled toward Jerusalem and people were flocking to see him. All along His travel route people were attempting to catch a glimpse of this supposed preacher and miracle worker. It seemed that the people were interrupting their normal routines of travel to satisfy their curiosity about this itinerate teacher. The ebb and flow of people that we normally would have encountered in our begging duties were seeking an encounter of a very different kind; they were looking for this Jesus. Soon, after a series of heated verbal exchanges, it was decided, by our group of leper nomads, that we really had nothing to lose by taking a good look for ourselves at this man. And indeed if the crowds were following him then it would be there at His public preaching events that we would have the best success. Thus, we started down the valley to the nearest village where it was rumored that he may be spending some time.

As we made our way along the main road, calling out "Unclean! Unclean!" we could see that the crowds of people were increasing, obviously something of real importance was taking place up ahead. Walking parallel to the road, but staying a safe distance from the actual graveled and foot worn surface, we followed the crowd as it snaked along toward its destination. Crying out "Unclean!" "Unclean!", while at the same time making the usual requests for help, we made our way just inside the village entrance. Crying out to make our presence known, we pressed in behind the onlookers to find a place well away from the main density of people. We chose to stay close enough to the low meandering rock wall that served as the village's simple and mostly inadequate protective barrier. This would give us a good chance to see this man close-up with as little interference as possible as he entered the village. It would also give us immediate access to a clear avenue of escape, if it proved to be that we were deemed unwelcome.

Soon amid the required calls of "Unclean!" "Unclean!" and the pitiful appeals for food and money, we could see the arrival of the much anticipated group of disciples and their leader, Jesus of Nazareth. At first, all of us just looked and watched, hoping to see some miracle or glorious demonstration of power. In this we were like everyone else who were pressing in around this preacher and his followers. As the disciples and their leader grew closer I could feel the deep stirring and emotion of my fellow lepers. Although they had previously been skeptical and negative about this preacher, now with his actual approach in view things began to change. Nervous movements, whispers, sighs and low urgent groans were beginning to break out from my nine companions, including myself. Although no formal plans had been made to approach this man from Nazareth, the possibility of receiving something of a miracle from Him seemed to generate a unified cry for help from all of us in our group. It was as if the pain of years of suffering could not let this opportunity pass by. Without the need of any words, our yearning hearts were saying that if miracles could happen and the mercy of God was truly available to those in need, well, now was the time to make our presence known and make our request crystal clear.

Without consultation, or coordination, our troop of desperate begging lepers began shouting at the man from Nazareth. Like a gushing spurting artisan well of emotion and desperation all of us joined in a unified chorus of sound.

"Help us!" one of my companions shouted.

"Please help us master!" another instantly added.

"Have mercy upon us!" another called out, yelling over the trailing sound of the others.

"Jesus, master, have mercy upon us!" others chimed in, adding to the reprise of voice and sound.

"May God help us!" others in the group were now calling out with strained and screeching voices and many tears.

With some standing, some kneeling and some laying painfully on their ragged torn clothing, all ten of us were shouting and calling at the same time toward the teacher. Face and mouth coverings could not muffle the intensity of our cries for help. It seemed, in fact, that as our petitions grew louder, our boldness increased. An explosion of emotion, pent up for years, was finally pouring from all of our wounded souls. Not only were we calling out at full voice capacity, many of our group were waving and thrusting their makeshift crutches, canes and walking sticks in the air to get the preacher's attention. In this grating and piercing display of anxiety, the entire crowd turned their gaze our way and were, for a time, silenced by our intruding persistence. Not only were they shocked by our presence, but they were shocked by our forward and daring behavior. Whether or not we would be greeted with approval or sternly rebuked never entered our minds. We only saw in an instant a change for our lives to change and so we called all the more loudly. It was in this brief silent moment of interlude that Jesus of Nazareth called back to us. His call toward us served to release another wave of surprise over the crowd. Not only had we interrupted the crowd's concentration toward this Jesus, but he had now taken the time to respond.

Douglas S. Malott

Chapter Five

The Miracle Arrives

I am not sure what the others expected would be His response, but I for one, thought that if a miracle were to happen, it would be a dramatic display of power with great fanfare and pomp. I suspected, in my imagination, that a cheer from the crowd would erupt as they witnessed the miracle take place before their very eyes. I am not sure where I had developed such expectation, but it just seemed to me that the chosen one of Israel would work with such dramatic expression to confirm his authority. Instead, this Jesus, gave us one simple instruction, one that we were already familiar with, but had never been privileged to experience for ourselves.

"Go and show yourselves to the priests." Jesus called back to us, as a matter of fact, without any noticeable display of power.

Taken back by the straight forward and quick response to our frantic calling and yelling, all of us looked with puzzled glances at each of the others in the group. Then with startled disjointed movement all ten of us awkwardly started collecting both our thoughts and our belongings. This command was traditionally given to any infected person whose skin condition had begun to heal or change for the better. It was done because it was required that the priest make a new examination of the affected skin and be able to issue an official "Clean" pronouncement of the individual involved.

This requirement we all knew very well and thus immediately were prompted to hold tightly to our meager possessions and start the long journey toward Jerusalem and the Temple of God. This would normally take a couple of days and so the quicker we could start the better. Like all of the others I made sure to gather my dirty travel bags, any of my soiled clothes that had been a part of my supply of necessities and especially any of the treasures that I had accumulated during my begging regimen. Bumping, pushing and stumbling over one another all ten of the men in my group started for the main road out of the area. With this sudden sense of hope all of us at once attempted to find the shortest distance to the village entrance and get our travel underway.

It was in this confusion and disorderly movement that I first felt and noticed something changing. While gathering up my things I had inadvertently exposed my right hand and arm as I rubbed and brushed against the bulky assortment of vessels and baggage that I now cradled against my chest. My first glance sent a jolt of shock through my entire being! I was so taken back that I was sure that my eyes were playing a deceiving trick in my head! Large areas of once scarred and ulcerated skin on the back of my hand and wrist and lower forearm were changing colors as I watched. Along with an ever so slight tingling sensation shades of white and soft pink were materializing in my skin from the former gray and black blotches! Dry and scaly patterns of broken skin were shriveling and disappearing even as I watched in utter amazement.

As you can imagine this was enough to stop me in my tracks. This completely captured all of my energy and focus. It was then that I could sense another very slight tingle and inching sensation across my chest, lower back and down over both of my legs.

It was not painful in the least but its gentle irritation told me something was taking place all over the diseased surfaces of my skin. As the strange sensations continued I had no choice but to send my menagerie of supplies tumbling back to the ground in front of me and take time to further investigate. Glancing up for just a brief moment I could see only the backs of my leprous friends moving down the road without me. I would soon join them, but for now I had to see more evidence of what was taking place as my miracle continued to develop.

Quickly I reached to the lower edge of my tattered tunic and raised it enough to look clearly at the side and back of my left leg. This limb had for some months developed the worst of my infection. Deterioration of the skin had progressed far enough that the underlying flesh was exposed and constantly oozing fluid. I was sure that it was only a matter of time before bone would begin to appear which would only add to the reoccurring bouts with pain and immobility. Because of this I had wrapped and rewrapped my leg several times a day in a hopeless attempt to slow my disease and guard my wounds from further damage. Now, as I peeled back the top layer of dirty make-shift bandages and gazed at my skin, the skin looked clear! Healthy pink shades of skin tone were spreading slowly through the once infected areas. There was no pain to be noticed and while flexing my muscles I could feel the strength returning to my entire left side.

Chapter Six

My Thankful Heart

The evidence was clearly mounting; I was experiencing my own personal miracle at the hands of this prophet and healer from Galilee! In the bustle and commotion of quickly moving bodies and the many stationary and stunned passersby, I knelt to the ground to make one last attempt at scooping up my haggard collection of personal treasures. I was alone now, alone with my thoughts as I gazed at the distant view of my friends leaving the area as fast as they could possible move.

"I should be doing the same thing!" I whispered to myself quietly.

"This miracle will no doubt earn me a life giving pronouncement of 'Clean' from the Temple priest", I continued to mumble under my breath.

"I dare not be delayed in my journey!" I argued with my inner self.

In all of my urgent conversation and self-made arguing, I found myself looking away from the road, away from my friends, away from the direction of Jerusalem and back toward the man from Nazareth. He was still standing among his followers and conversing with them and the many admirers that remained in the village. He seemed very engaged and focused on those who surrounded him and no doubt each of them would take exception to being interrupted by an outsider. But now, as the full weight of my healing settled over me, I knew I could not leave without seeing Him personally. Jerusalem, the Temple and the priests would have to wait! *I had to talk with this man, sent from God!*

Again, I let tumble to the ground my belongings and my worn and used treasures. The only thing that mattered now was to get to this Jesus of Nazareth. My miracle and its reality were driving me toward this man. As everyone and everything else faded into the background of my view, I moved directly toward this miracle man and his disciples. After taking my first few steps I could no longer conceal by joy. It was as if my steps, in His direction released a pressurized fire of gratefulness from the depths of my soul.

"May God be praised", I yelled at the top of my lungs, startling those who were closest to me.

"Glory to the God of Israel, His mercies endure forever" I continued sputtering and shouting as I made my way closer to the Nazarene. Now, a small opening was developing in front of the Master as the surprised crowd watched me close the distance between us.

"Salvation has come to this sinner! Jehovah has mended my brokenness!" I gasped as I stumbled and fell to my knees and then to my face at the feet of this Jesus.

"Thank you, my master, thank you! May the God of heaven be praised!" I finally acknowledged with my face buried in the rocky ground at our feet.

I was now overcome with tears of joy and waves of

emotion that rippled across my skin from head to foot. I had come, along with hundreds of others, to watch this man from a distance. I had come as just another curious onlooker. Only very remotely had I thought of ever being a part of some demonstration of power at the hands of this Jesus. And honestly, if questioned beforehand, it would have been easier to believe that someone else might receive healing rather than myself. I simple came to watch, yet He had restored my life and my future with just one spoken sentence. In the crush of emotion and spent energy I could do nothing but keep my face to the ground and bask in the glow of the fresh realization that just as my life had been given a 'death' pronouncement eleven years ago, now, it had been given a 'life' pronouncement; pronouncement that would again change me forever. As I gathered my natural senses about me, wiped hot tears from my cheeks and began to lift myself from the ground I heard again that familiar voice make another inquiry.

"Were not 10 cleansed?" Jesus spoke again.

"Where are the other nine? Didn't any return to give glory to God except this foreigner?" Jesus continued saying.

It was Jesus addressing the crowd which remained standing above and around me. No one responded to his questioning. Even I was too overwhelmed to say anything. I did not know exactly where the other nine had gone. I only supposed that they had run off in their excitement toward Jerusalem. No doubt, they, like me, were probably overwhelmed by their own emotions and caught up in the thrill of traveling to Jerusalem to confirm their healing. As for me, however, I had come to one conclusion only. I knew that I could not have left without expressing my deep and sincere gratitude for what had happened.

Now, as the crowd, silenced by His questions, again began to converse among themselves, Jesus turned directly to me and with His piecing gaze and authoritative voice and mannerism said simply two more things to me.

"Get up and go on your way. Your faith has made you well." He spoke to me.

Having given this simple declaration to me, he moved on with His disciples and the mass of onlookers that had accompanied Him to this location. I stood silently for some time not knowing entirely what to do next. In my indecisiveness I chose to just watch as Jesus of Galilee made his way out the village entrance and down the valley road in the direction of Jerusalem.

Chapter Seven

The Final Report

Very soon the reality of my new found freedom stirred me into motion. As this Jesus of Nazareth had instructed, I would go to Jerusalem and report to the priests for an examination. This would give only secondary confirmation to what I already knew first hand: that my leprosy was gone! But, first, there was a destination that must be my priority. I would travel back to my village and announce my miracle to my family and along with some of them make that repeat trip to Jerusalem and to the Temple of God. This time without the accompanying cloud of dread and fear that had been our hated companion eleven long years ago.

From Capernaum south and then west toward the Great Mediterranean Sea, I made my way back to my village. This route was very familiar, as numerous begging trips had been made by the leper group of which I was a part over the previous eleven torturous years. Never in all of those years had we been able to cover the distance in less than a full day, since most of us were constantly nursing our leprous wounds and also attempting to plead for help at every opportunity that presented itself.

This trip however would prove to be completely different. From the moment that I took my first steps back on the road from Capernaum and away from the Sea of Galilee, my energy seemed to increase. Soon, as the reality of my healing made its full impression on my thinking, I dutifully and systematically began to discard my tattered and torn clothing. It was no longer needed to mark me out among the crowds. I could now walk quietly without any cry of warning or alarm. As well, for the first time in these many years, I would be able to expose my skin to the warmth of the sun and the wisps of breeze that cycled down the foothills around me and through the valley.

As I walked my hurried pace, my attention was drawn again and again to the fresh pink and rosy tones of my own skin. It was all I could do to remain in motion and not stop to stare at myself. The tension between needing to proceed as fast as possible and the desire to slow my pace enough to admire my healed condition was a welcomed and new dilemma during the entire journey back to my village. Indeed it was a great gift to wrestle with such a joyous inner struggle.

Not more than a quarter's day walk had transpired before I saw the outer reaches of the village. Moving with clear and purposeful determination I made my way through the eastern gate of the small and low protective stone wall that surrounded the main living area. With only a few turns through the narrow and angled pathways I was brought to my family's dwelling. In previous years, had I made such an approach, everyone within hearing distance would have been alerted to my presence by calls of "Unclean! Unclean!" And of course recognizing me under the many layers of bandages and required skin coverings would have been next to impossible for both family and friends.

Today, however was a different day! Several neighbors were already following me at a curious distance struggling to make sense of what they were seeing. Others, who had not joined the small procession, but who were obviously remembering who I was, stopped their activities to stare as I plodded by each of them. Arriving at the edge of the small courtyard that served as the entrance to several small dwellings, including that of my own family, I simply stood for a few minutes taking in the scene and atmosphere. Never in my wildest dreams would I have thought that a day like today could happen, and yet here I was, about to unleash a flood of raw emotion and joy over the people who meant the most to me in all the world.

As I stood watching from the dusty pathway and preparing to make my entrance, movement developed under one the overhanging tarps that served to provide shade for those working at the front of the house. It was my mother! She was carrying a large water pot to the courtyard to be filled later at the community well. For the moment, as was the custom, she would make several trips in and out of the house with as many water pots as were available to be later loaded on a small cart to make the short trip to get fresh water. In an instant I knew what I would do to announce my arrival.

"Is there some way I can help you with those water pots?" I asked, making little effort to disguise my voice.

"Thank you for your kind offer sir, but I have several able bodied men here in the house to help me finish the task," she replied without looking up to see who had made the offer, as my voice was yet unrecognized.

"I would consider it an honor to be included among those able bodied men, if you would not mind," I continued with my surprise offer.

This response brought a slow but calculated turn to my mother's still beautiful but aging face. The inquisitive look on her face seemed to say that somehow the sound of my voice was now becoming familiar and beckoning. As she turned to gain a full view of who was making this odd request, a sudden burst of awareness spread over her entire countenance. All at once, tears and laughter and joyous screams erupted from her heart. The surprise at seeing me almost sent an empty pot crashing to the ground from her straining arms. In an instantaneous movement of shock and discovery, she put down the water pot, rolled it with a hollow 'clunk' to the others sitting nearby and began running toward me.

Holding up the lower front side of her robe with one hand so as to not trip and reaching out toward me with the other she moved like a gazelle over the short distance that remained between us. It was only within a few short yards of reaching me that she stopped to take a good look at my appearance. The initial surge of emotion had propelled her toward me without any clear assessment of my leprous condition. Only after almost reaching me had she realized that, as before, caution had to be taken so as not to touch my infected skin. As she came to an uncomfortable stop to finally look me over, the expression of surprise and unbelief was more than I could take.

"Mother, it's alright!" I called out to her.

"I have been cleansed of my leprosy! I am healed and there is no longer any danger!" I called again to her as her stood motionless before me.

"I have met the man they call Jesus and his words have made me well", I continued, now with a rush of tears beginning to cascade down my own cheeks.

At the sound of my last words, relief settled over my

mother's entire appearance and so with one last thrust of short and energetic steps, she was in my arms weeping and laughing and kissing my neck. As the embrace continued in its intensity and emotion, one by one, friends, family and neighbors slowly gathered around to see up close what they had heard me announce just minutes before. Soon the entire collection of humble dwellings had emptied their people into the courtyard and the narrow street to witness my arrival, view the glorious family reunion that was taking place and to hear my story of meeting Jesus at Capernaum.

The next day was spent gathering supplies and making preparations to travel to Jerusalem. I was determined to get to the Holy City and the Temple as soon as I could to have the last vestiges of leprosy's curse removed from my life. Making our way south from Samaria to Jerusalem would again take a two day journey, but this time the journey was rife with laughter and hope. This time the ominous view of the Holy City, with its ancient walls and tall regal gates stirred deep feelings of praise and gratefulness in my spirit.

After entering the city again from the north side and making our way up to the broad expanse of the outer courtyard of the great Temple of God, I proceeded back to the side wall under a portion of King Solomon's portico to wait for an available priest. There, as before, selected priests appointed for such duties were waiting to examine any concerned individuals. I found a place in line again and listened and watched as the many people ahead of me were examined and declared 'clean' or 'unclean'. The atmosphere was full of emotion and fearful energy. But this time as I watched, my spirit was soaring with expectancy and energy.

As my turn came and I slowly removed the upper portion

of my tunic to allow the priest to have a clear unhindered view of my skin, I could see the complete absence of concern in the eyes and on the face of the Levite who quietly looked over my once irritated skin. As his eyes closely examined my skin, his mannerisms became very succinct and abbreviated. Unlike my encounter of eleven years ago, there was no concern displayed and without delay or hesitation the priest made his pronouncement.

"This man is clean! Whatever skin condition was previously present is now gone. He is declared clean!", called the priest to those who were with me and to the crowd that spread out around us.

In the thrill of my new found health and the enthusiasm of the prospect of my newly secured future, I left the Temple with my family surrounding me and joyfully made my way back to the North Country of Samaria and Galilee. With eleven years of physical and emotional prison behind me, I was ready to make my dreams and future a reality. Little did I know that in the blindness of my own personal ecstasy, I was oblivious to the turmoil and hatred that was surfacing in Jerusalem and other parts of Israel concerning the Man from Galilee. This turmoil and hatred would result in the death of this man, the man who's simple and direct words had healed me of my leprosy.

Postlude:

Those glorious days are now a year past and I am still consumed with gratefulness and thanksgiving. As I convey this incredible account to you, I am filled with the joy of each and every day going about my daily routine of working, helping my friends, reconnecting with my family and even preparing for what was once the unthinkable; my upcoming wedding day. In the same way that this cool and striking water invigorates and stimulates my senses as I am washed by it's flow, so my heart and mind have also been washed. Thinking back to those early conversations with my leper begging partners, I did not know who this Jesus might be or whether or not His message was true. I could only hope it might be true. Now, having thrilled to the freedom of being healed, being normal, healthy and productive, I have no doubts at all. For me, this Jesus is indeed the Messiah! He is indeed my Messiah!

The End.

Douglas S. Malott

Story Five

The Glorious Shipwreck on the Island of Malta

Douglas S. Malott

The Glorious Shipwreck on the Island of Malta
Based on Acts Chapter 27

Prologue

The year was approximately 62 A.D. and Paul the Apostle had been placed under arrest by the Roman authorities in Jerusalem. This had taken place due to the fact that Paul had been beaten by Jewish zealots and accused of violating several of the sacred Hebrew laws in regard to the Temple. His arrest was ordered to protect his life from those in Jerusalem who saw him as a serious threat to Judaism. While under arrest it was discovered that numerous of the zealots had taken a vow to kill the Apostle at the first opportunity. With the plot to murder him uncovered, it was decided that the best option for his safety would be to move him by armed guard to the city of Caesarea Maritima on the Mediterranean Sea.

Once in Caesarea Maritima numerous formal complaints were registered against Paul by the Priestly delegation that had followed him from Jerusalem and several hearings were aired before the Roman magistrates. Seeing that he risked being sent back to the hostile atmosphere in Jerusalem, Paul appealed his case to Caesar and then was ordered to Rome under the supervision of a certain Centurion named Julius.

The amazing story of this voyage to Rome and its detour to the Island of Malta is recorded in the 27th chapter of the Book of Acts of the New Testament. In the story that follows, the amazing account of this dangerous and life-threatening voyage is told by the Roman guard who was assigned to transport Paul to Rome.

Chapter One

The Contrary Winds

My name is Julius. I am a Roman Centurion charged with the unpleasant task of transporting prisoners from the territory of Israel to Rome. This was one aspect of military service that was most unenjoyable as it was a thankless and dangerous business. Although it can be seen as an honor to be entrusted with prodding criminals to their final destination for trial, imprisonment or perhaps execution, I was not enamored with the duty. One particular trip to Rome, however, turned out to be a voyage of a lifetime as it brought me face to face with a new religious sect taking root in the Roman Empire and one of its most notorious leaders. These who were called 'Christians' and adhered to the teaching of one Jesus Christ of Nazareth were led by several individuals, one of which was a Paul of Tarsus. He was considered to be an Apostle of this group and who, as it turned out, would be placed in my charge for an infamous sail to Rome. This is my story.

I, Julius, had serviced the Caesar for many years, in fact, I served several different Caesars, while fulfilling my sacred tribute to the great Roman Empire. However, I would have much rather spent my time in the field in the action of war or at least training for it as my primary focus. It was for such action that I had been trained. But now with most of the empire's boundaries secure, the Roman legions were given the task of keeping the peace and enforcing law and order, particularly in areas like Judea where many of the Jews were intent on overthrowing Rome's control and supervision. It was in this capacity that I had been assigned to the city of Caesarea Maritima, on the beautiful shores of the Great Mediterranean Sea. The Emperor himself had dispatched me to this area directly from the royal palace in Rome where I had been serving him as one of many personal assistants. As a centurion, I had 100 of Rome's finest soldiers serving under me and together we provided a formidable force when gathering up malcontents and other prisoners.

It was in conducting these duties that I first encountered the man, Paul of Tarsus. While gathering and processing prisoners for our eventual sailing trip to Rome, I had been contacted by the officials of Governor Festus and given one more common criminal for transport by ship to the courts of Rome. Little did I know, at the time, that this man Paul was anything but a common criminal! In fact, I would come to believe, through a series of extraordinary events, that he was truly a man of God, dedicated to his faith and no doubt wrongly accused and wrongly sentenced to jail. Coming to this conclusion would be no easy task, but rather the terrifying process of a very long, arduous voyage, a devastating storm at sea and the experience of barely escaping with my life from a shipwreck! In the end, after seeing what I saw, there was no doubt in my mind about who he was or what God he served. I only wished in the end that I had not needed to deliver him to Rome, especially since his God had delivered me from the throws of death.

Making arrangements to transport prisoners required several weeks of preparation and searching. With no military vessels available, I was forced to secure a transport ship from the port of Adramyttium, that was scheduled to make several stops along the east and north shores of the Great Sea as it made its way closer to Rome. The Adramyttium ship was a medium-sized ship and designed to carry cargo on short distance voyages along the coast, thus escaping the dangers of the open sea. As was usual for these kinds of voyages, we would travel as far as we could on the available ship and then need to make arrangements later for another ship to carry us further up the coastline toward our final destination.

We left Caesarea and made a short trip to the City of Sidon, just up the coast a half days voyage. Here we waited while cargo was exchanged and additional provisions where secured. It was here that I first encountered several of Paul's friends. These so called 'Christians' were very gracious to their friend and his traveling companions, requesting permission to house this Paul until the time arrived to set sail. Not seeing any real threat from these kindly people I sent Paul and his small partly, along with two soldiers, to stay in the city until we were ready.

In two short days we put out to sea; captain, crew, Paul with his companions, the other prisoners and my restless soldiers ready for a longer trip. Sailing west directly out of port we encountered contrary winds, making our hope to skirt under the island of Cyprus only a dream. Immediately we were forced to track with the winds and sail along the northern shore of the big island. Perhaps if I had been paying attention to the signs, I would have seen in this first change of plans a more foreboding warning. But since I did not, we simply plunged ahead toward a strange and frightening destiny. After sailing, with much resistance, through the open sea off the coast of Cilicia and Pamphylia, we reached the port of Myra in Lycia.

It was here that I was forced to contract another ship, since our previous one was not on schedule to meet our transport needs to Rome. A quick survey of the available ships brought me to an Alexandrian ship with a huge cargo of wheat and miscellaneous supplies. These ships where well known in the area since our entire empire depended on their sailing from the south country where grain was plentiful. These ships of Egyptian origin were strong and capable but were not designed for long open sea sailing, so our hope was to glide along the north shores, around the tip of Achaia and into the safer waters of Italia. As fate would have it, this was not to be. If I thought we had encountered contrary winds earlier in the week, what was about to blow over us in the few weeks ahead would be nothing short of a small hurricane!

Leaving Myra, attempting to continue west, we were met immediately with the same contrary wind opposing us. After sailing many days with great difficulty as far as the Cnidus Peninsula and not being able to approach the city for portage, we were forced to give in to the wind and sail south and under the Island of Crete just off of the city port of Salmone. At this juncture the wind became even more intense and opposing, threatening to push us ever closer into the open sea to the south. With yet more difficulty we drove and propelled our modest ship under the eastern tip of Crete and dove directly to safety in a place called Fair Havens near the city of Lasea. Even with our ship safely in port, the strong winds and repeated rain storms buffeted the small bay and made staying longer a serious trial of patience.

Chapter Two

Promise of Survival

It was here I made a most regrettable decision. Bringing the Captain, the owner of the ship and several crew members together, I discussed the options that we faced. There were three at this stage of the voyage. We could stay here for the winter and put back to sea in about three or four months or we could attempt to push to the north on the edge of the open sea and try to make it to the southern tip of Greece where we might find more favorable winds. Lastly, we could make a quick run up the coast to the more suitable port of Phoenix and over-winter there. As the discussion was developing and opinions were being exchanged, the pressure of our lost time became obvious to us all. If a decision was to be made in favor of continuing it needed to be made now. We simply did not have the luxury of wasting any more time. It was at this point that the prisoner Paul stepped into the conversation from somewhere in the hold of the ship. I had not seen him for several days since he had been preoccupied with his religious habits of fasting and prayer. So I was surprised to see him up on deck and a bit taken back at his boldness to approach us, given his chains. But, it was from this breaking of the fast that Paul approached us with a somber warning.

"Men", he said, "I can see that this voyage is headed directly toward damage, heavy loss and possibly loss of our very lives", he stated soberly to us all.

"In my opinion, staying here is our safest option", he concluded, hoping we would listen well.

The captain and the owner, being overly sensitive to their need to deliver cargo and also not wanting to winter where it would be unsafe for their ship, insisted that effort be made to get to Phoenix and there spend the rest of the winter. I was not sure of how much stock to put in this prisoner and his warning, seeing that he had little experience in these kind of matters; so, although a bit reluctant, I agreed that we should make the attempt to sail the half day trip into Phoenix. What should have been a simple half day trip turned out to a nightmare of a journey and made me wish many times over that I had listened to Paul.

On the morning that we were ready to sail, a gentle south wind sprang up from across the bay and we were certain that our fortunes had changed, so we weighed anchor, set the sail, turned the rudder and headed out along the shore of Crete toward the west. It appeared that this was exactly what we wanted and needed to reach the more secure harbor of Phoenix. Our hopes were short lived, however. As we progressed, inching our way up the coast, suddenly a strong 'northeaster' rushed down from the steep slopes of the island and struck us broadside. The island of Crete possessed many majestic mountains and massively rugged and jagged peaks and although beautiful to behold, they could become savage in their ability to promote typhoon-like winds and weather along the coast. It was just one such blast that had now caught us.

We were trapped in the grip of a snarling wind. As the 'northeaster' had pushed from the mainland up and over the high peaks of the island of Crete, the fierce pressure had created a firm funnel effect that was driving us out to the open sea. Our last chance of making landfall safely was soon passing by us on the right in the form of the small island of Cauda. Seeing its welcoming shores encouraged everyone on board that safe harbor was within reach. This was not to be, however, as soon we could only silently watch as the island sped by us and offered no help for our panic-stricken craft. Our only option now was to give way to the wind and let the ship ride with the waves as the blustery coiling force drove us out to sea. It was at this juncture that we decided to pull the skiff aboard. It had been faithfully trailing behind us at the end of a long tether for all these weeks in case we needed to abandon ship. Since that was now a distinct possibility, we elected to keep it tied to the top deck. With much labor and struggle, we were barely able to gather in the drenched and snapping tether line and bring the small craft onto the deck. With the skiff now secure, it became clear that every ounce of strength would need to be expended to stabilize the vessel by taking every available rope, tackle and cable and start girding the ship's timbers, planks and cargo against the wind and waves.

    No sooner had we secured the skiff and cargo but a fear of running aground swept over the captain and crew. In their minds nothing was more fearsome than the possibility of being pounded into a sand bar and having the ship become an open target for the howling wind. In that kind of sandy death trap, the ship would be pounded and broken into a thousand pieces. It was decided that in order to help prevent this, a large drift anchor was dropped off the stern of the ship to hold us back against the driving wind and current.

    Hour after hour we were being mercilessly and severely battered by the storm. It was decided later in the day because of this relentless thrashing and after the battering became almost unbearable, some of the heavier cargo had to go. We began to jettison piece after piece of cargo, hoping to lighten the load and increase our chances of saving the ship. On the third day of our ordeal we had no choice but to begin throwing the ship's gear overboard as well, since it added too much additional weight to the ship. Painstakingly the crew, amidst crashing waves and jarring wind blasts, disassembled the hoist mounts, the boom arms, the pulley supports, and the extra mast and sail sheeting and let it all wash overboard. The days had turned to weeks and at this point in the torment, we had not seen the sun by day or the stars by night during any of this time. We were just being driven along in a misty grey darkness that seemed to wrap all around us.

After nearly two weeks of this torture it appeared that all was lost. I regretted daily my decision to attempt the trip in the first place. All on board were either exhausted, sick, frightened to the point of despair or all of these things combined. A sullen misery and hopelessness stood watch over every soul; it was expected at any moment that we would be tossed into the sea to be lost forever! It was in the middle of this plague of despondency, while several of us were trying to make a final assessment of our plight, that we were approached by the prisoner from Judea. I was not expecting him to add anything constructive to our conversation so when he started by pointing out to us our obvious mistake in leaving Fair Haven, I was not impressed. I certainly agreed with him at this point about our blunder but to hash it over again seemed of little use now. I was beginning to feel flashes of anger at his interruption when what he said next caught me off guard and turned my head in utter disbelief.

Chapter Three

Thrown Upon the Rocks

With the wind howling and the fresh salt spray of crashing waves biting at each of us, this prisoner Paul pleaded.

"Men," Paul said, "I urge you to take courage, because there will be no loss of any of your lives, but only the loss of the ship. For this night an Angel of the God I serve has appeared and stood by me with confirming words. The Angel said, 'Don't be afraid, Paul. You must stand before Caesar. And, look indeed the Lord has graciously given you all those who are sailing with you," he continued.

We were staring blankly at Paul not really comprehending his words as he continued with boldness.

"Therefore, take courage all of you men, because I believe God that it will be just the way it was conveyed to me. However, I must warn you that we will need to run aground on an island to be spared!" He finished.

I could not believe my ears! This Paul of the Hebrews had seen an angel who had promised us our lives! The God of Israel had decided to be gracious to us all and keep us alive? Those around me made little reaction to this declaration, largely because we were all completely out of strength and tired to the bone. But, of course, given the complete lack of other options, we soon became very inclined to believe any such word that gave us even a shred of hope. With reluctance but nothing better to offer, we listened intently as Paul's specific instructions were rehearsed among us.

As we were approaching our fourteenth day of drifting and being driven by the wind in the Adriatic Sea, several of the sailors thought we were approaching land. The sound of the wind and the waves seemed to take on a different sound throughout the early evening with the distant reverberation of surf coming over the surface of the water to greet us. With this new development, the sailors scrambled to take a sounding of the water depth and as the line and lead weight were lowered overboard we found it to be 120 feet deep. This in itself told us that we were not in the open sea now but moving over more shallow waters. It would be the next sounding, however, that would determine whether or not we were moving closer to land or farther away from it. After sailing a little farther along in the tempest, the second sounding was made and this time the line measurement found it to be 90 feet. We had lost about 30 feet of depth over just a few minutes time. This indeed meant that we were NOT moving out over deeper water but about to be blown directly into some type of land mass. By this time we could only hope that it wasn't some rocky place that would tear the bottom from the ship and leave us swimming for our lives!

Hoping to prevent a meeting with rock and waves, the order went out to drop anchors from the stern of the ship. Four huge lead anchors were lowered from their support lines into the spraying waves and water out the wide back of the ship over the top of the rudder. This we could hope would somehow slow our progress and keep us from being hurled forward against the island or land mass that we were sure was fast approaching. As the anchors and ropes disappeared in the surf behind us, we settled our mind and hearts as much as we could, praying and waiting for daylight to break.

It was several hours into our waiting that I was alerted to an angry commotion on the starboard side of the ship. Moving quickly to the side of the craft, with sword in hand, I caught sight of several sailors trying to lower the rescue skiff into the sea in order to make an attempt at escaping. Apparently these sailors had pretended to be throwing additional anchors off the bow in order to make a sudden rush to the skiff to try and get it overboard. The noise of the turmoil brought soldiers and others to the deck to see what was happening, including the Apostle.

'Unless these men stay in the ship they cannot be saved!' Paul immediately called to me and several soldiers standing with me.

With his words echoing in my brain, I gave the order to leave the skiff where it was and commanded the desperate soldiers back to their stations. As I did so, with lightning fast reaction, three other soldiers dashed to the edge of the ship through the driving rain toward the skiff, but instead of securing the skiff, they drew their swords and slashed at the ropes holding the skiff to its mooring. The skiff, now cut loose, slid along the decking and banged its way over the side of the rail and dropped silently into the raging sea below. There was no escaping now.

Either Paul's God came through or we were doomed to the mercy of a deadly storm.

Daybreak did finally come and with that Paul stood again to address us all, urging us to take some food in order to have enough strength to survive the rest of our ordeal. Reaching for his own bread and taking several bites he gave thanks to his God in front of us all assuring each of us that not a hair of our heads would be lost! This was indeed a heartening sign to behold. Paul's confidence seemed to bolster our resolve; soldier, prisoner and sailor alike. Indeed all 276 of us in the ship began to eat what was left of our rations with the expectancy of somehow being able to wrestle our way to safety through the clawing sea water. As strength slowly returned to both body and mind, it seemed that one last thing could be done to further lighten the ship for its final pitch toward shore; so with one last effort we all began to send container after container of grain into the salty expanse that surrounded us.

As more of the daylight spread over us and opened some of the clouds above us, in the distance was revealed a land mass directly off our bow. We were traveling in a direct path toward its shore being pushed and pummeled by the nagging wind and spray of the fierce storm. The land was not recognizable nor was any other familiar landmark visible but there did appear to be a small beach that might afford us a chance at a direct run up on the sand. With that observation confirmed, the four anchors dragging off the stern of the ship were cut loose and left in the sea behind us and the ropes that had held the rudders in position were loosened. Then the foresail was hoisted into the wind and with a mighty jerk the ship lurched forward toward the beach.

All of us could do nothing but watch. The foresail strained with the full force of the wind in its spread. The water crashed and slapped at all sides of the ship sending giant finger like waves gushing across and over the deck. We watched and waited and held on for our very lives. Suddenly we were all thrown forward in the hold and along the railing. We had struck a sandbar and the ship was jammed fast into the hidden wall of sand and was not moving. In the moments after this reality settled on us, we were shaken again by several explosive thundering breakers that came slamming into the stern of the ship. Again they came crashing into and over the high stern section. As the pounding continued, the planks, decking, back railing and joists began their inevitable dismemberment and the entire stern of the ship began dropping piece by piece into the water. There was now no other choice but to abandon ship and throw ourselves into the sea.

Chapter Four

Every Man Overboard!

As was standard procedure in emergencies like these, several of the soldiers began drawing their swords to kill the prisoners lest they swim to shore and escape. I understood their actions but given the ordeal of the last three weeks and the presence of Paul among us, I could not bear to see this happen.

"Stay the sword!" I yelled at the top of my lungs to insure no violence would befall the prisoners.

"Ignore the prisoners for now and make for the surf!" I cried out against the driving salt water and wind.

Immediately the swords were released and with precious little time to spare since looking quickly out over the faltering and dying vessel, we had little time to deal with the possibilities of escaping prisoners. Immediately I ordered all who could swim to jump overboard and make for shore and for the others who could not swim to grab planking or debris from the ship and float their way to the beach. At that command, people began jumping, diving and dropping into the cold salty sea. From every direction individuals were entering the water around the ship, some splashing frantically as they began to swim, other desperately clutching debris or pieces of the ships planking to stay afloat. Of course, the sailors who were accustomed to the sea quickly responded, prisoners and soldiers, on the other hand, were more trepid in their effort, but given the options they too found their way into the water and headed toward shore.

This entire frantic action was taking place as the vessel repeatedly shook and quivered from the continual pounding of the waves and huge breakers reaching high in the air that continued crashing and rolling over the deck. As I surveyed the scene around me, I could see the many dim, vague and shadowy figures all fighting their way through the force of the spray and wind to get to the ship's side, make their way over the railing into the water and as far away from the stricken vessel as possible. At last, with most of the crew and passengers on their way into the deep, I climbed over one of the ship's side rails and standing with my back toward the dying ship, held myself out over the watery deep and plunged into the sea. The cold shock of hitting the water sent my heart and mind reeling. Icy needles jabbed at my clothes and skin as I fervently flailed both arms forward to make headway toward the shore. Through the spray and waves that were washing over my back, head and face and over the bobbing and darting pieces of debris in front of me, I could just make out in the distance a slender slice of a sandy beach and so with all my might I headed for it.

Madly, I flailed my arms and hands attempting to make headway in the boiling surf. Rolling in the waves, spitting out water that attempted to fill my mouth and dragging drenched and thus heavy clothing and of course my weaponry, I plowed through the white and grey water. As I made headway all I could do was rehearse the words of Paul the prisoner in my mind, **'not a hair on your head will be lost'**.

Making one's way through bubbling, frothing, boiling surf is no easy task. As I struggled forward against the waves I wondered about the others. Were they making it onto the beach? What of my soldiers? Would the promise of this Paul of Tarsus hold them afloat amidst these crushing breakers? And what of the prisoners; including Paul himself, how were they to find their way through this surging water with arm and leg wounds still fresh from the constant chafing of their previous chains? Some perhaps still in chains! Alas, there was not time to dwell on the others; I had to make my survival the priority for the time being.

Finally, after what seemed a very long and arduous time, I could feel the roll of the surf under and around me pushing me forward toward more shallow water. Soon I felt the rubbing of sand and pebbles against my hands and feet as I moved along. What a sense of relief and hope simultaneously flooded my mind as first one foot then the other found firm support under the rolling white-topped waves. I staggered up the gradual slope of the beach as I found my footing and with the help of both arms and hands crawled and lurched out of the sea on to the beckoning sand. Immediately my mind went to the so called Apostle Paul and his prediction. He had been right, at least for me, and although cold, bruised and disoriented, I was safe on the beach, given another chance at life!

Kneeling in the soft wet sand and feeling the hard rhythmic slaps and blows of the waves from behind brought my thinking back to the moment. Now, I was eager to see what was happening around me. Turning to look behind me, back over my right shoulder, I could make out the twisted remains of the ship in the distance. It was still forged into the sand bar and being beaten and broken by huge breaking waves, each one sending shock waves through the remaining timbers and deck supports of the ship's stern. With each pounding breaker the ship was pushed deeper into its sandy grave while what was left of its seaward stern was being lifted and smashed over the rest of the ship's rear decking. I was sure from the towering size of the waves and the cracking sounds that blasted toward me that it would not be long before a final death blow would envelope the ship and nothing would be left of its rugged frame.

As I watched the ship in the distance, I could see in the foreground where sand and sea met, all along the bubbling wave line, small splashes of white water and tiny staggering figures struggling up out of the surf, like so many tiny creatures coming up out of their graves. Soldiers, sailors and prisoners, strung out all along the beach line were crawling their way up the wet sandy surface of the beach to safety and a future. Indeed as I focused my attention across the small but open beach, many more figures than could be easily counted came into my view. From my vantage point it now appeared that perhaps a majority of our passengers had survived the wreck. In fact looking up and down the beach, indicated to me that perhaps all of them may have survived! As this idea settled over me a sudden burst of unsuspected gratitude swept over my soul and, without warning a gentle piercing jab of conviction gripped me as the validity of the prisoner Paul's words came into focus in my mind. This God, who Paul claimed as his own, whom he served, had chosen to rescue an entire shipload of strangers out of the most extreme of circumstances; one that proved to be a harrowing brush with death due to my own crucial lapse in common sense.

Walking slowly up the sandy beach, wet to the core but still clutching my sword, I was eventually joined by the other survivors who staggered and slogged their way toward me. One by one, each of my soldiers checked in, then, the ship's captain and crew began finding their way to our location. In addition, the large assemblage of prisoners in my charge, also took their turns stepping out of the light rolling fog and joined us. As each additional person was stepping forward to meet us on the upper portion of the beach, we soon realized, as I had done earlier, that ALL on board had survived and each of us would live to tell our stories.

As the crowd grew larger and all of us at once began reciting our individual ordeals to each other, the topic of conversation gradually turned toward the one person that all of us had on our minds and that all of us were looking for; this Paul of Tarsus. With several loud and piercing inquiries called out over the gathering group, Paul, reluctant as usual to be in the center of attention, finally made his way through the exhausted and emotionally spent passengers. Walking gently and deliberately Paul stepped around some who were kneeling, some who appeared to be praying, and others who were flat on their face against the sand and still others who were softly crying in relief. He moved out from the crowd toward the center of our large uneven circle of weary people and found a position alongside me.

As everyone slowly became aware that Paul was now standing before us, a quiet reverence prompted by deep respect broke through the late morning fog and settled over the entire group. Whether we were just too tired to talk, or the shock of our ordeal was still gripping us, or we were simply in awe of the gracious miracle we had just experienced, I was not sure. I only knew that for several minutes no one wanted to speak. For these several minutes we held our peace and remained silent in the moment. With the wind continuing to blow, rain pelting us from all directions and the still present but distant echoes of the surf devouring our ship, we quietly paid our respect to Paul of Tarsus and his God. It was only when several men close to the Apostle had moved to his side and began thanking him that the respectful silence was broken.

Chapter Five

The Unexpected Welcome

I am sure this hallowed moment would have continued for some time longer had our concentration not been interrupted by the sounds of voices and commotion coming to us from the tree line above the beach. A few quick glimpses up the sand to the dark line of trees and vegetation that marked the end of the beach's upward slope, forced us to realized that not only were we all alive on an unfamiliar beach but we were also being greeted and welcomed by the inhabitants of the island. Out of the tree line came dozens of shadowed and unfamiliar native people. They were carrying torches and large bundles of wood and brush as they moved toward us. At first glance we were not sure of their intentions but soon it became clear that this was a welcoming party not one intending to harm us. As they made their way closer to us, we could see that they were preparing to start a large bonfire on the beach by which we could warm ourselves. This was almost a dreamlike conclusion to a horrifying three week voyage that had taken us to the brink of death and back.

As the 275 other survivors, plus myself, did our best to gather around the huge bonfire that quickly blazed into a comforting furnace of fire, we soon learned about our precarious landing spot. As these hard working native people rushed to and fro to make us comfortable on the damp beach, we were told that we had made our way to the island of Malta. With this information in hand, it now became clear that our ship had been driven by the currents and prevailing winds away from the Fair Havens harbor on the Island Crete to the west and with a force of monstrous proportions had aimed us directly at the southern tip of Sicily. Since we had been forced to give the ship's rudder over to the mercy of the wind and waves, our continued westerly direction had brought us to a rugged portion of sea water at the eastern end of the island of Malta. It had been there that the converging currents had pushed our vessel into the sand and rocks at the edge of this secluded bay and beach.

As we stood around the fire, attempting to shake the cold from our chilled bodies, we soon discovered that numerous of the local people had been watching our ship struggle against the storm for many hours before it made its way into the large sandbar that guarded the opening to the bay. They, unknown to us, had been preparing for our arrival for several hours, hoping the ship would make it through the narrow opening to the bay. As the storm had increased in its intensity, this possibility had faded quickly and it had become clear that our ship would find its way to a most unfavorable end. It was then that these people, who knew the results could be disastrous, had perched themselves under the protection of the shoreline trees and waited at the edge of the beach to watch the outcome of our ship's final voyage and be ready to help any survivors. And so now, having survived our plunge into the deep, we stood, with only the clothes on our backs as our possessions, being warmed by a fire provided by an unlikely group of friends.

Before much time had passed, the roaring crackle of the fire was beginning to dry our clothes and provide enough additional light to help us see the faces of the kind-hearted Maltese people more clearly. As the fire continued to burn and sizzle in the misty salt air, and we mingled and talked with our friendly hosts, many of us who had regained enough strength to do so, ventured up and down the beach area collecting brushwood and scattered wood for the fire. With the trauma of our survival still shrouded over us and with such a large number of our people who needed to be warmed, a steady supply of wood and burnable items was needed. So all of us, who were physically able, including myself, joined the search to see to it that we had a continuing supply of fuel. And of course, without hesitation, the prisoner Paul joined the processional of wood gatherers and brought his several loads of wood to dump in the growing bonfire.

Chapter Six

The Miracle Fire

Over the next few hours a steady stream of people moved to and from the huge bonfire that now lit up much of the beach area depositing their supplies of wood into the popping flames. Given our otherwise hopeless situation, both the gathering of wood, which now included some that had been torn from our ship, and the busy walking of the beach served to restore our focus and give us an immediate purpose. It was in this seemly harmless but much needed cycle of movement that a final poignant development brought our three week long ordeal in the sea to an end. And it all came about because of the need to supply fuel for our fire.

Paul the Apostle had made several short trips along the sandy beach to collect wood like everyone else. Each time, like all of the others, he would collect his share of wood and then proceed to toss the miscellaneous pieces out onto the already burning pieces that had been previously deposited. In one such cycle of work, Paul stepped closer than usual to the flames to empty his arm full of kindling for the fire. It was in this precarious reach out over the flames that a vicious attack occurred.

Reacting to the heat of the fire and the sudden shock of having been moved from his hiding place among the various pieces of brushwood, a hidden viper, made his frantic move. Unseen by any of us, it's coiled and venomous body sprang toward Paul. Without warning, in an instant of time, the viper's two upper fangs found their mark in the soft tissue of the back of Paul's hand and helped secure its grip as its lower jaw clamped tightly to his palm and hung in midair next to the blazing fire. As Paul stepped back a few short steps from the edge of the fire, with the snake still dangling from his hand, the reaction from the local people was almost instantaneous. The sight of such an event brought a predictable recoiling from all who were close enough to see what was happening, but particularly from the island people who viewed the episode as a sign from the gods.

"This man is no doubt a murderer!" one local man was heard announcing to the others who were watching.

"In spite of the fact that he has escaped the sea, the goddess Justice, does not allow him to live!" he continued to pronounce to the witnesses.

With this new stir of commotion suddenly swirling around him, Paul simply stepped back to the edge of the cracking flames and with one quick and violent shake of his wrist, sent the viper twisting and writhing through the air into the hottest portion of the fire to be instantly consumed by its hot coals and heat. As the viper thrashed hopelessly in his fiery grave, Paul quietly stood by the flames doing nothing more than giving his slightly wounded hand a gentle rub and massage. The local native people were now all the more curious as they watched Paul standing calmly beside the fire warming himself with all of the others. It was clear from the way these people continued to stare and watch that they expected something dramatic to transpire immediately. Whether or not they expected Paul to fall to the wet sand beneath him and die or perhaps witness the swelling and disfiguration of his bitten hand, I was not sure. It was clear, however, that having the viper suddenly attack Paul was being interpreted as a sign that Paul deserved to die.

With this perception firmly in their minds, all who had seen the viper's attack expected Paul to suffer immediate retribution. But as the minutes passed and nothing happened and then as the minutes turned into many hours, the mood and demeanor of the local people began to change. The longer that Paul showed no signs of negative affect, the more the people began to gather around him. Still watching with great curiously and intrigue, they who in the beginning had recoiled, were now being attracted to him. Soon the verdict was changed. A man who could endure the attack of a poisonous viper and simply shake it off into the fire and not experience a single negative affect was not a criminal but rather a god.

In the three weeks of sailing that I had observed this man, I had been impressed with his gracious demeanor, his polite manner (even though he was required to be in chains as a prisoner) and his devotion to the Hebrew God. I saw no evidence that he was a god, nor did I see any evidence that he deserved to be in chains. Although I had discounted his advice and dismissed his council due to his inexperience in dealing with the unpredictable business of commercial sailing, he had been respectful and prayerful in response. And of course his predictions of our traumatic but safe arrival on this unexpected island only confirmed the power of the God he served and the gracious mercy by which we were all saved.

So, although I could not believe this Apostle Paul to be a god, I certainly had come to respect and believe in his God and in his faith. And now with the local people opening their hearts to this man from Israel, there was no doubt in my mind that our extended visit on the island of Malta would provide my prisoner Paul a grand opportunity to bring the message of his faith to all of us who had survived and to the gracious people of Malta.

The End

ABOUT THE AUTHOR

Douglas S. Malott currently resides in Spokane, Washington with wife, Patti, where he was born and raised. Doug and Patti have been married for 38 years and have 4 grown children, one really great son-in-law, along with two wonderful grandchildren. Doug has been in the ministry since 1980 and has been the Senior Pastor at The Rock of Ages Christian Fellowship since 1982. Pastor Malott has his Bachelors' Degree in Business and Education from Whitworth University, in Spokane Washington, and his Master's Degree in Biblical Studies from Trinity College of the Bible and Seminary in Newburgh, Indiana.

Made in the USA
Middletown, DE
08 September 2022

73490043R00106